T0304558

THE
GURU
GAP

Also by David McKnight

The Power of Zero
Look Before You LIRP
The Volatility Shield
Tax-Free Income for Life
The Infinity Code

THE
GURU
GAP

How America's Financial Gurus Are Leading You Astray, and How to Get Back on Track

David McKnight

Matt Holt Books
An Imprint of BenBella Books, Inc.
Dallas, TX

The Guru Gap copyright © 2024 by David McKnight

All rights reserved. No part of this book may be used or reproduced in any manner whatsoever without written permission of the publisher, except in the case of brief quotations embodied in critical articles or reviews.

Matt Holt is an imprint of BenBella Books, Inc.
10440 N. Central Expressway
Suite 800
Dallas, TX 75231
benbellabooks.com
Send feedback to feedback@benbellabooks.com

BenBella and *Matt Holt* are federally registered trademarks.

Printed in the United States of America
10 9 8 7 6 5 4 3 2 1

Library of Congress Control Number: 2024033593
ISBN 9781637746622 (hardcover)
ISBN 9781637746639 (electronic)

Copyediting by Michael Fedison
Proofreading by Karen Wise and Jenny Bridges
Text design and composition by PerfecType, Nashville, TN
Cover design by David McKnight
Printed by Lake Book Manufacturing

For my family.

CONTENTS

FOREWORD

Household risks change after retirement. Yet, for many financial gurus, there is still a lack of recognition about how the post-retirement phase differs after individuals have stepped out of the workforce. In 2024, there is no excuse for these shortsighted attitudes, as we have known at least since the 1990s how different retirement is from pre-retirement.

For one clear example, David McKnight explains how William Bengen's research first published in 1994 showed how market volatility lowers the sustainable spending rate from an investment portfolio relative to what one might expect when simply assuming that an average investment return is earned every year. Yet Dave Ramsey continues to espouse the idea that an 8%

withdrawal rate from investments in retirement is safe because, according to him, the "stock market averages 12% per year."

Things simply don't work this way. Retirement requires different thinking. Households save and accumulate when working to build an asset base that will fund their retirement goals. While working and saving, the financial world has generally emphasized the need to construct diversified investment portfolios relying on stocks to outperform bonds to support asset growth.

In retirement, households seek to sustainably support their lifestyle for as long as they live, to maintain liquidity to cover unexpected expenses and contingencies in retirement, and to provide a legacy for the family or community. They must do this without their work paycheck.

Meanwhile, retirees face new risks, key among which are longevity risk and amplified market volatility. Longevity risk is the possibility of living longer than planned, which could mean not having sufficient resources to maintain one's standard of living. Market volatility is the risk that poor market returns are realized. Retirement distributions amplify market risks, as it is harder for an investment portfolio to recover from a market downturn in retirement because the retiree is selling shares and taking distributions from the declining portfolio, leaving less available to benefit from any subsequent market recovery.

What David refers to as the "stock market approach" for generating retirement income—the one preferred by the gurus discussed in this book—takes the same strategy espoused during the pre-retirement savings phase and blindly applies it to retirement.

These financial gurus maintain an investments-oriented focus for both the accumulation *and* retirement life phases. With investment-oriented strategies, retirement risks are generally managed by spending as little as possible in retirement. Longevity risk is managed by assuming a long life, and market risk is managed by assuming poor market returns. Planning for worst financial cases can make retirement a more expensive proposition in terms of requiring a larger amount of assets to feel comfortable that the retirement plan will work.

I was part of a research team that created the Retirement Income Style Awareness™ tool, which consistently shows that only about one in three Americans is comfortable with basing their retirement income strategy on this purely investments-based approach. Two out of three Americans prefer approaches that create protections for assets earmarked for essential retirement expenses, or are more comfortable with strategies that commit to solving their lifetime spending needs. These protections are available through contracts from insurance companies that pool longevity and market risks across a broad collection of customers.

This is why David's critique of the guru way is so important. The gurus' methods simply do not resonate with the preferences of most Americans in retirement. David outlines the importance of at least considering tools such as annuities and permanent life insurance in the retirement planning tool kit, as they can provide valuable protections for retirees who may otherwise be paralyzed into underspending in retirement because they worry about outliving their investment assets or not having the resources to pay for contingencies like long-term care.

David also properly emphasizes the important role that a Roth conversion strategy can play in retirement.

This is something I've analyzed extensively, and the tax planning chapter in my *Retirement Planning Guidebook* is the longest. It's problematic that Dave Ramsey recommends avoiding Roth conversions once one is less than five years from retirement and to never pay the taxes on Roth conversions from the tax-deferred retirement account. Both points are wrong. First, it is generally the early retirement years that provide the best opportunity to convert funds at lower effective tax rates. And though I do prefer to pay the taxes from elsewhere, the idea that one should never pay the taxes on a Roth conversion through a distribution from the tax-deferred account simply is not true. Yet I see online discussion forums where people quote Dave Ramsey on these points as reasons to avoid Roth conversions, quite possibly to the overall detriment of their retirement. The tax code and long-term tax planning are complicated, and simple knee-jerk reactions based on intuitive assessments can easily lead to wrong conclusions.

For these reasons, I applaud David for writing this book and for helping to combat the oversimplified messages from the gurus that tend to get the most airplay and attention from the public. Hopefully this book can help bring better financial planning practices to a wider segment of our population.

Wade D. Pfau, PhD, CFA, RICP
Author, *Retirement Planning Guidebook: Navigating the Important Decisions for Retirement Success*
Cofounder, Retirement Income Style Awareness, LLC
Professor of Practice, The American College of Financial Services

1
The Guru Gap

Financial guru Dave Ramsey once received a call on his popular show in which a retiree asked if he could increase the withdrawal rate on his savings from 4% to 5% to do a little more traveling in retirement. His financial advisor had advised against the higher spending, but the caller was anxious to hear Ramsey's opinion. Ramsey responded by saying that if the caller simply allocated 100% of his retirement savings to stocks, he could grow his assets at 12% per year and therefore take sustainable withdrawals of not 5%, not 6%, but *8%* per year for life! If a 12% annual return was possible, and Ramsey assured him it was, then an 8% withdrawal rate was perfectly reasonable. Relieved, the caller thanked Ramsey and hung up, fully prepared to *double* the rate of withdrawal on his retirement savings.

This was an extraordinarily surreal moment for me because I fully understood that Ramsey was overstating sustainable distribution rates by 100%. The gold standard for sustainable withdrawals since the early '90s has been a paltry 4% per year. Based on the latest economic data, some experts have even revised it downward to as low as 3%. Dumbfounded, I took to the internet to try to understand the genesis of Ramsey's 8% withdrawal rate stance. In the process, I learned I wasn't the only one who was flummoxed by Ramsey's stratospheric withdrawal rate assumptions.

As I dug deeper, I learned that Ramsey had a now-famous kerfuffle with a band of Certified Financial Planner® professionals on Twitter in which they censured him for his advocacy of the 8% withdrawal rate. Hundreds of thousands of Monte Carlo simulations and reams of academic data, they insisted, confirmed that the highest sustainable distribution rate in retirement was, at most, 4%. And by adopting an 8% distribution rate, Ramsey's listeners risked depleting their retirement savings far in advance of life expectancy. The implications for Ramsey's listeners, these CFPs concluded, were potentially cataclysmic.

Soon, Wade Pfau, a PhD economist from Princeton, and one of the world's leading experts on sustainable withdrawal rates in retirement, got in on the conversation. In a series of articles that critiqued Dave Ramsey's 8% withdrawal rate dogma, Pfau demonstrated how it leads to a catastrophically high rate of failure. For a 65-year-old with a 100% stock portfolio who wants their assets to last a full 30 years in retirement, an 8% distribution rate would prematurely deplete their assets an astounding 63% of the time.

Was Dave Ramsey unaware of the academic studies that supported the traditional time-tested standard for sustainable withdrawal rates? It's possible, but not likely. If he was, in fact, familiar with the studies, then why would he recommend a withdrawal rate that was so radically out of line with consensus? There are five reasons why this is likely the case, each of which sheds light on Ramsey's financial planning worldview and reveals a worrisome disregard for time-tested financial planning principles.

1. He's Not a Financial Advisor at Heart

The first reason is surprisingly simple: Dave Ramsey is not, at his core, a traditional financial advisor. At least that's not the background from which he emerged. In 1988, Ramsey became over-leveraged in a variety of real estate investments and ended up filing for bankruptcy. Two years later he formed the Lampo Group, a financial counseling service that specialized in helping consumers eliminate debt using his controversial "debt snowball method." Ramsey's debt-counselor approach to finances operated outside the framework of traditional financial planning. As a result, he didn't marinate in the financial orthodoxy that might have at least reined in some of his more bizarre, math-averse takes on sustainable retirement planning principles.

2. Ramsey's Antiestablishment Persona

The second explanation for Ramsey's "outside the box" retirement advice is that he has intentionally cultivated an antagonistic relationship with the traditional financial planning community. Near the end of the exchange with the caller at the beginning of this chapter, he explained why the financial advisor was uneasy with a distribution rate higher than 4%. "He's a financial planning lemming," Ramsey explained. "He's just following the crowd." The inference was that the caller's advisor was part of the stodgy, mainstream financial establishment and therefore incapable of thinking in unconventional ways. Further, the advisor's reason for discouraging higher withdrawal rates, Ramsey suggested, was financially motivated. If the client spent more than 4% of his portfolio per year, then the advisor would have less money to manage, and would therefore *make* less money.

In fact, during the feud with the Certified Financial Planners over his 8% withdrawal recommendation, Ramsey tweeted,

I can help more people in ten minutes than you can in your entire lives. You're snobs because you don't help regular people.

The dig at traditional financial planners was clear: the only measuring stick for good financial planning advice should be the extent to which it "improves" the lives of a broad swath of America.

3. Expanding His Empire

To understand Dave Ramsey's often contentious relationship with the mainstream financial community, you must also understand his overarching objective: expanding the Ramsey empire. Don't get me wrong, there can be little question that Ramsey *is* sincerely motivated to get Americans out of debt and turn their lives around. When you watch *The Dave Ramsey Show*, his conviction leaps off the screen. However, there's no denying that Ramsey is a shrewd marketer and his driving motivation is to expand his following. To do so, he must draw a stark distinction between himself and mainstream financial planners by consistently questioning their creativity and motivations. By doing so, he drives a wedge between investors and their advisors and slowly, but inexorably, draws them into his tribe. This approach was on full display in the exchange I referenced at the beginning of this chapter.

4. The "One Size Fits All" Advisor

The fourth reason Ramsey's approach runs afoul of convention is his need to appeal to a large and diverse audience. To gain *and* retain listeners from as many demographics as possible, he must preach an inclusionary doctrine that's short on details and long on pithy axioms. Regardless of their financial profile, listeners must feel like Ramsey is speaking directly to their personal financial situation. Ramsey accomplishes this by preaching a watered-down, albeit folksy, one-size-fits-all financial planning dogma that appeals to a broad array of Americans. If Ramsey were to say that a given retirement solution worked in scenarios A, B, and C, but not in D, E, or F, then he'd underscore the need for a customized, tailored plan that draws upon niche planning principles—which he rejects. Now, you may point out that Ramsey routinely refers his listeners to his well-vetted, SmartVestor Pro advisors. But alas, these advisors are expected to parrot the Ramsey approach to retirement planning or risk excommunication from the program.

5. Your Dreams *Can* Come True!

Finally, Dave Ramsey's success hinges on his ability to convince millions of Americans that it's a lot easier to achieve their retirement dreams than they might think. Consider the following. If Dave Ramsey were to advocate a 4% withdrawal rate and a more conservative (but realistic) 8% growth rate on investments, then he'd be sending a clear and unequivocal message to his audience: *You will never become financially independent.*

Let me illustrate. Let's say you're 30 years old, want to save $500 per month, and you anticipate growing your retirement savings at 8% per year. By the time you reach 65, you will have accumulated $1,078,176. If you subscribe to the Four Percent Rule, you'd be able to safely withdraw $43,127 your first year of retirement, adjusted every year thereafter for inflation. If you account for a 3% inflation factor over those 35 years, that's only $15,327 of spending power in today's dollars. These types of anemic results would hardly fire the imagination of Ramsey's listeners.

However, if you subscribe to the Dave Ramsey school of retirement projections, the picture improves considerably. If you could instead grow your money at 12% per year (as Ramsey suggests), that same $500 monthly savings will net you $2,900,779 by age 65. That's a $1,822,603 improvement! And if instead of withdrawing 4% of your assets per year, you pump that up to 8% as Ramsey recommends, you're now looking at a $232,062 distribution day-1 of retirement, adjusted every year thereafter for inflation. That's a whopping $82,471 in today's dollars! That's a 538% improvement over the mainstream financial planning approach! When coupled with your Social Security, that may just be enough to meet your lifestyle needs over the arc of a full 30-year retirement!

These types of results are enough to energize even the most undermotivated of Ramsey's followers. It could even inspire them to take their first step toward securing their financial independence. After all, anything the mind can conceive *and believe*, it can achieve.

THE GURU GAP

Now, I freely acknowledge that Dave Ramsey has helped millions of Americans who are mired down in debt and sliding quickly into insolvency. If you make $50,000 per year but spend $60,000, Dave Ramsey is likely the person you *should* be turning to right about now. In fact, when I served as the leader of a congregation, I kept a copy of Ramsey's *The Total Money Makeover* on my shelf for congregants who struggled to stay on top of their finances. I say this in all sincerity: Ramsey is to be commended for the outsized impact he's had on Americans who are drowning in debt and struggling to get ahead.

But while Ramsey's advice is precisely what millions of high-debt, low-income Americans need to hear, it is ill fitted to the disciplined, sophisticated investor. In fact, Americans who have worked hard and saved well risk losing hundreds of thousands of dollars while exposing themselves to an array of insidious risks over the course of their retirement journey by heeding Ramsey's advice.

The difference between the financial advice you're likely to receive from Ramsey and the type of customized, math-based advice your retirement plan requires is what I call "The Guru Gap." And this is a gap into which hundreds of thousands of good investors unwittingly fall by embracing Ramsey's math-be-darned approach to retirement planning.

A CUMULATIVE GAP

But alas, this is not intended to be a book exclusively about Dave Ramsey. The broader story is he's hardly the only guru who succumbs to some or all of the five above-mentioned failings. Other famous gurus such as Suze Orman, Clark Howard, Ken Fisher, and Ramit Sethi dispense similar paint-by-numbers planning strategies that create guru gaps of their own. Now, this isn't to say that their advice is uniformly bad. I could cite a number of instances where their viewpoints align very closely with my own. However, their goal of appealing to a broad, disparate audience often taints their advice with a vagueness and superficiality that contributes to a massive, *cumulative* guru gap. And this is the gap into which seasoned investors whose situations call for niche expertise and customized financial plans often fall.

WHY I WROTE THIS BOOK

The purpose of this book is to draw a stark contrast between generalized guru advice, which is often short on details and long on platitudes, and the specific, proven, math-based advice that I outline in my best-selling books *The Power of Zero* and *Tax-Free Income for Life*. Why am I comparing these gurus' principles with my own books instead of a popular, mainstream financial planning tome? At the center of my retirement planning approach is the core belief that tax rates, even 10 years from now, are likely to be dramatically higher than they are today (more on this in chapter 3). Any retirement approach that doesn't account for the strong likelihood of higher future taxes is, by definition, inadequate and incomplete.

While I *will* offer sharp critiques of these gurus' strategies and opinions, this book is *not* intended to be a personal attack. Rather, it's a good-faith attempt to foster dialogue around how Americans can harness math and time-tested financial planning principles to ensure that their retirement savings last through life expectancy.

In the next chapter, I'll discuss the standard guru advice when it comes to making sure your money lasts as long as you do, a theme I touched upon at the beginning of this chapter. I'll then contrast that approach with the proven, math-based advice that not only mitigates longevity risk, but also eliminates a subset of risks that longevity risk amplifies. In chapter 3, I'll make the case that tax rates in the future are likely to skyrocket and demonstrate how traditional gurus often give this insidious threat short shrift. I'll then lay out the most current math-based strategies that can help shield your hard-earned retirement strategies from the impact of higher taxes. In chapter 4, I'll document the unjustified hate campaign financial gurus have waged against traditional cash value life insurance and show how math and history vindicate its role in a balanced, comprehensive approach to tax-free retirement. And finally, in chapters 5 and 6, I'll give you two case studies that compare and contrast the gurus' paint-by-numbers approach to retirement planning with a customized, math-based, Power of Zero strategy that can shield you from the most pernicious retirement risks and dramatically extend the life of your retirement savings.

2

Solving Longevity Risk

According to nearly every study on the subject, the American retiree's greatest fear is running out of money before he runs out of life. You know, living too long and dying broke? In the mainstream financial planning community, this threat is referred to as *longevity risk*. It's an especially insidious risk because it magnifies the likelihood or consequences of a subset of risks that could land you in the poorhouse years in advance of life expectancy. These risks include *sequence of return risk*, *withdrawal rate risk*, *long-term care risk*, and *inflation risk*.

Before I contrast our gurus' approach to mitigating longevity risk with the Power of Zero approach, I'd like to give you a quick overview of each risk. Doing so will provide you plenty of motivation to purge them from your retirement picture.

Sequence of Return Risk

Sequence of return risk relates to the order in which you experience returns on your investments. If you experience a series of negative returns early in retirement, it could send your portfolio into a death spiral from which it never recovers. This could force you to run out of money years in advance of life expectancy and eke out an existence on Social Security alone.

Withdrawal Rate Risk

The second sub-risk that gets magnified by longevity risk is withdrawal rate risk. This is the risk of taking unduly high distributions from your stock market portfolio and running out of money before you die. To be clear, longevity risk doesn't *increase* the likelihood that you'll succumb to withdrawal rate risk, but it does magnify the consequences of running out of money far in advance of life expectancy.

Long-Term Care Risk

Long-term care is one of the most insidious retirement risks because it can force you to burn through a lifetime of savings in just a few short years. To drive home the implications of this risk, I typically have the following conversation with my clients. In this example, we'll call them Mr. and Mrs. Jones.

Me: Mr. Jones, you know I love you, right?
Mr. Jones: Yes, Dave, I know you love me.

Me: I do love you, but you're better off dying than needing long-term care.

Mr. Jones: (in a concerned voice) Why's that?

Me: Because at least if you died, Mrs. Jones here is the beneficiary on all of your investment accounts. And while we would miss you terribly, life for her would carry along relatively unchanged.

Mr. Jones: (Raises his eyebrows.)

Me: But if you didn't die . . . if you almost died, and ended up needing long-term care, then most of the money she was planning on spending in retirement now gets earmarked for the long-term care facility. Mrs. Jones would get to keep one house, one car, a Minimum Monthly Maintenance Needs Allowance (MMMNA) of about $2,500 per month, and about $130,000 of cash. So, what was shaping up to be a perfectly rosy retirement for Mrs. Jones turns into basic, bare-bones, subsistence-type living. And, of course, the converse is true should Mrs. Jones end up needing long-term care.

So, what does longevity risk have to do with long-term care risk? Not surprisingly, the longer you live, the higher the likelihood you'll end up needing long-term care. This, in turn, increases the likelihood that you'll burn through your retirement savings to pay for it. Not exactly how you or your spouse anticipated spending your golden years in retirement.

Inflation Risk

Let's face it, money is valuable because it's scarce. And the more you print it, the less scarce it becomes. Unfortunately, the US government has increasingly turned to money printing as a way to either bridge its budget shortfalls or respond to economic emergencies like COVID-19.

As our nation slides further into insolvency (more on why this is happening in chapter 3), you will see the federal government increasingly turn to money printing, or what it euphemistically refers to as "quantitative easing," to shore up its fiscal outlook. Unfortunately, this means that inflation risk will only grow more ominous as time wears on.

What does inflation have to do with longevity risk? The connection should be clear. The longer you live, the greater the risk that inflation will erode your spending power. This increases the likelihood that you'll prematurely deplete your assets before you die.

THE GURU WAY: THE STOCK MARKET APPROACH

The gurus' preferred (and only) approach to mitigating longevity risk, and by extension the four sub-risks I described above, is what has come to be known as the *stock market approach*. This involves building up a huge pile of money by the time you retire and then constraining yourself to a modest annual withdrawal rate. This became popular in the early '90s as a result of the research done by MIT-trained financial advisor William Bengen. He was appalled by the willy-nilly approach that investors took to drawing down their retirement savings. Americans were spending down their portfolios at 6%, 7%, and in some cases even 10% per year. If you didn't know what constituted a reasonable withdrawal rate assumption, you simply asked yourself the question: What has the stock market returned historically? And whatever answer you came up with, that was your acceptable rate of distribution in retirement. If the market had returned 7% historically, that was a perfectly reasonable rate at which to draw down your stock market portfolio.

The Four Percent Rule

Given the catastrophic implications of running out of money prior to life expectancy, Bengen wanted to create more certainty around what constituted a sustainable withdrawal rate. So, he began to conduct a number of empirical simulations based on the history of stock market returns. He used variables such as withdrawal rates, stock-bond allocation, rates of return, and length of retirement to create success rates (likelihood of not running out of money before you die) around various distribution percentages. And what he learned shocked him to his core. Ten percent distributions had catastrophic failure rates. Even 5% distributions failed over half the time. He finally determined that, given a 60/40 stock-bond split over a 30-year retirement, you could take a 4% distribution rate and maintain a high likelihood that your money would last through life expectancy.

Bengen's stark data around distribution failure rates

is why mainstream financial gurus, with the obvious exception of Dave Ramsey, have rallied around what came to be known as the Four Percent Rule.

Clark Howard

Nationally syndicated radio show host Clark Howard has long been an unapologetic fan of the Four Percent Rule. In fact, Howard's team was so bent on demonstrating the dependability of the rule that they performed Monte Carlo simulations of their own. Here's what they found:

> Our work recreated Bengen's study with retirement withdrawals beginning every year from 1929 to 2009. This is 82 separate retirement starting points. We used actual market data until 2017 and ran multiple simulations with historically conservative average return estimates after that: 5% for stocks, 2% for bonds, and 3% for inflation figures.
>
> Here is a brief rundown of our findings:
>
> - 70% of the time (58 of 82 scenarios) retirement funds lasted 50 years or more.

- *30% of the time, the money "ran out" with the worst-case scenario in our study being 29 years.*

Our conclusion: Yes, the 4% Rule still works.[1]

After rerunning Bengen's simulations with prevailing economic data, Howard and his team were more than satisfied with the ongoing reliability of the Four Percent Rule.

Ken Fisher

Ken Fisher, the CEO of Fisher Investments, is so confident in the Four Percent Rule that he wrote an article countering a Morningstar report that warned of the Four Percent Rule's early demise. Morningstar claimed that in their most recent simulations based on updated economic data, the Four Percent Rule was successful only 75% of the time. Fisher's website lists several reasons why you should *still* put your trust in the Four Percent Rule:

---

1. Wes Moss and Sally McDonald, "The 4% Rule: Why It Still Makes Sense for Retirement," Clark Howard, January 7, 2019, https://clark.com/personal-finance-credit/budgeting-saving/4-percent-rule-retirement/.

One, if a quarter of simulations ran out of money, that means three-fourths of them didn't, rendering a roughly 75% probability of not outliving the assets. Two, a modest failure rate isn't exactly a breaking development . . . There are always risks and unknowns in investing, but we aren't inclined to buy the this time is different *argument we have seen since this report broke.*[2]

Even if the Four Percent Rule has become slightly less reliable in recent years, Fisher maintains, it's still the single greatest way to purge longevity risk from your retirement picture.

Problems with the Four Percent Rule

Even though the Four Percent Rule is endorsed by nearly every mainstream financial guru, it is not without its drawbacks. As it turns out, it has a series of glaring shortfalls that can trip up even the most circumspect

2. Fisher Investments Editorial Staff, "Digging Deeper into the 4% Rule's Alleged Demise," Fisher Investments, February 15, 2023, https://www.fisherinvestments.com/en-us/insights/market-commentary/digging-deeper-into-the-4-rules-alleged-demise.

of investors. What follows is a brief overview of each of those shortcomings.

Shortfall #1: It's Expensive

If you can only ever withdraw 4% of your day-1 balance in retirement, adjusted every year thereafter for inflation, you'll have to accumulate a massive amount of money by the time you retire. To understand precisely how much, simply divide your desired pretax lifestyle by your maximum distribution rate, in this case 4%. For example, if you want a lifestyle of $100,000 in retirement, divide $100,000 by 4%. The formula looks like this:

$$\frac{\$100,000}{.04}$$

When you divide $100,000 by 4%, you find that you will need to have saved $2,500,000 by day-1 of retirement. And if, like most Americans, you aren't on track to accumulate the required amount, you'll have to resort to one of five unsavory, angst-inducing alternatives: save more, spend less, work longer, die sooner, or take more risk in the stock market. I'll discuss each of these five options (plus a possible sixth alternative) in more detail in chapter 4.

Shortfall #2: Inflexible Distributions

The second failing of the Four Percent Rule is that it leaves little margin for error. If in any given year you take 5%, 6%, or, heaven forbid, 8% (that's right, Ramsey, I'm talking to you!), you undermine the mathematical framework that undergirds the Four Percent Rule and dramatically increase the likelihood that you *will* run out of money before you die. For the Four Percent Rule to work as intended, you must obey it with absolute precision. And that's difficult to do over five years, let alone a 30-year retirement.

Shortfall #3: The Need for Discipline

To be a successful investor, you must, as the age-old axiom says, buy low and sell high. What plays out in the lives of everyday investors, however, is just the opposite. Fueled by emotions, investors tend to buy investments at their peak and then bail out when the market begins to fall. Unfortunately, this perverse form of market timing is starkly at odds with the math that upholds the Four Percent Rule. For the Four Percent Rule to work, you have to keep your money invested through good markets and bad. Even when the theater is on fire and people are stampeding toward the exit, you have to keep your money in the market. If you're constantly shifting your money to cash when things get hairy, you won't earn the robust returns required for your portfolio to last through life expectancy.

The real problem with emotion-fueled market timing is it requires you to be right twice: once when getting out of the market and once when getting back in. This is difficult for trained fund managers to pull off, let alone the undisciplined, neophyte investor. The Four Percent Rule demands discipline, not just over several months or a few years, but over the arc of a full 30-year retirement. And sadly, it's nearly impossible for do-it-yourself investors to marshal this type of persistence.

Shortfall #4: The Illusion of Liquidity

Let's say that through a combination of discipline and sacrifice, you *do* save the money required by the Four Percent Rule. Let's call it $2,500,000. According to the

Four Percent Rule, you could withdraw $100,000 your first year of retirement, adjusted for inflation every year thereafter. Here's the problem: it's very easy to mistake this massive pile of money for a slush fund or discretionary account that can be accessed on a whim. It's like leaving a massive cookie jar on your kitchen counter. If it's always within reach, it's just a question of time before you grab a cookie and take a bite! But you must remember that every last one of those dollars has been claimed by the Four Percent Rule. And if you start taking distributions in a willy-nilly or haphazard way, then you once again violate the complex math that upholds the Four Percent Rule. This dramatically decreases the likelihood that your money will last through life expectancy.

THE DANGEROUS TRUTH

So all this begs the question: If the Four Percent Rule is rife with pitfalls, why do all the mainstream financial gurus put so much trust in it? Are there simply no other alternatives? The truth is, gurus (again, with the exception of Ramsey, of course) endorse the Four Percent Rule because the only other alternative is unimaginable. It's so far outside the one-size-fits-all framework around which they've built their financial planning worldviews that it must be rejected out of hand. What am I talking about? The most unthinkable, verboten of all alternatives: annuities.

Solving Longevity Risk Through Annuities

Now, before you tune me out and cast this book aside, know that if you reject the underlying premise of annuities, you are simultaneously rejecting the mathematical principles that undergird Social Security and that company pension you may be planning on receiving. In their most basic form, annuities are the only financial tool that allows you to *completely* purge longevity risk from your retirement picture. I'm not talking about a 75% or even an 85% success rate. I'm talking 100%. Here's how it works. You hand a liquid portion of your retirement savings over to an insurance company in exchange for a stream of money that's guaranteed to last so long as you're on this side of the grass.[3] Insurance companies can make these guarantees through a concept known

---

3. Guarantees are based on the claims-paying ability of the insurance company.

as risk pooling. They know that some people in the risk pool will die prematurely while others will live longer than average. To the extent that you live longer than the average person in the risk pool, you avail yourself of what are known as *mortality credits*. These mortality credits are what ensure that you'll keep on receiving that monthly paycheck until your last, dying breath.

The Gurus' Stance on Annuities

All the gurus we've heretofore discussed heap unmitigated hatred upon annuities and deride them as the hallmark of financial hacks and scammers. But none of these gurus harbor more seething contempt for annuities than the CEO of Fisher Investments, Ken Fisher himself. Over the last 20 years, he's become the self-appointed leader of the anti-annuity crusade. He's even trademarked the phrase "I Hate Annuities."[4]

In fact, Fisher once put out a video in which he famously said, "I would die and go to hell before I would

---

4. Fisher Investments, https://www.fisherinvestments.com/en-us/personal-wealth-management/your-financial-goals/grow-your-wealth/asset-types/annuities/i-hate-annuities.

sell an annuity."[5] He then went on to list eight reasons why you should never consider an annuity and instead hand your money over to, you guessed it, Fisher Investments.

When you scratch just below the surface of Fisher's claims, however, you find that they're at odds with both math and reams of academic data. The truth is, annuities can help you purge longevity risk from your retirement picture far more effectively and for much less money than the Four Percent Rule. To demonstrate this, I took a stab at debunking every claim in Fisher's now-famous video. Doing so, I believe, goes a long way toward bridging that vast chasm between what the gurus recommend and what your retirement plan requires to successfully purge longevity risk from your golden years.

Criticism #1: "Most annuities have nosebleed-level fees."

Okay, do annuities have nosebleed-level fees? For the most part, the answer is no. In fact, other than Variable

---

5. Fisher has since removed this video from YouTube, but all eight segments of the original video can be seen in my own video critiquing his anti-annuity stance: https://www.youtube.com/watch?v=Gw8XAlX9rSw&t=16s

Annuities, most of them don't have any fees at all. I'm talking Fixed Annuities, Indexed Annuities, Deferred Income Annuities, and Single Premium Immediate Annuities. If the insurance company tells you you're getting a guaranteed $1,000 per month for the rest of your life, that's exactly what you're getting. No fees ever get deducted from that stream of income.

Further, if your most important retirement goal is to make sure you never run out of money, then you should compare the costs of the stock market approach that Ken Fisher recommends and a guaranteed life-time income annuity approach. What you'll find is that annuities mitigate longevity risk a lot more effectively and a lot less expensively than the Four Percent Rule.

Take, for example, a Single Premium Immediate Annuity. If a 65-year-old needed guaranteed lifetime income of $40,000 per year with a guaranteed 3% annual adjustment for inflation, that would require an initial deposit of around $675,000. Under the Four Percent Rule, you'd need much closer to $1,000,000 to realize that same level of income, and even then, there's no guarantee your money would last through life expectancy.

The problem is that when Ken Fisher says that "most

annuities have nosebleed-level fees," he's actually referring to Variable Annuities.[6] And to be sure Variable Annuities do have high fees. But by failing to distinguish which type of annuity he's referring to, he wittingly impugns them all. And the unsuspecting viewer is left to believe that all annuities have stratospheric fees and should be avoided at all costs. Ken Fisher and his fellow gurus' antipathy toward annuities fails to account for the reality that the Four Percent Rule approach to mitigating longevity risk is substantially more expensive—and riskier—than a financial alternative they universally condemn.

So, what do we make of this claim? *Misleading*.

Next, Ken Fisher claims that consumers don't know exactly what they're getting when they purchase an annuity.

Criticism #2: "Annuities don't do what the customer thinks they do."

Having interacted with countless investors over the last 25 years, I can assure you they know precisely what they're getting when they purchase an annuity: a

---

6. Fisher Investments, https://www.fisherinvestments.com/en-us/personal-wealth-management/your-financial-goals/grow-your-wealth/asset-types/annuities/variable-annuities

stream of income that's guaranteed to last for the rest of their lives. As I said at the beginning of this chapter, running out of money prior to death is the average retiree's greatest trepidation. They fear it more than death itself! Annuities help assuage that angst. When they hand a portion of their liquid retirement savings over to an insurance company, they receive a guarantee that those fears will never be realized. So long as they're on this side of the grass, they'll keep receiving that retirement paycheck, and they'll keep having to find a way to spend it.

So, what do we make of this claim? Also *misleading*.

Next, Ken Fisher claims that annuities are problematic from a tax perspective.

Criticism #3: "Annuities have tremendous tax problems."

Do annuities *really* have tremendous tax problems? Well, the majority of annuities are funded with money from IRAs and 401(k)s and are treated under the exact same section of the IRS tax code. So, if Fisher is concerned with how annuities are being taxed, he should be just as concerned with how the billions of dollars in IRA money he manages are being taxed. And Fisher has *every* reason to be concerned. You see, when you put money into tax-deferred accounts like 401(k)s and IRAs, it's like going into a business partnership with the IRS and every year they get to vote on what percentage of *your* profits *they* get to keep. Not a very good business partnership, if you ask me. So, you could have $1,000,000 in your IRA, but unless you can accurately predict what tax rates are going to be in the year you take that money out, you don't really know how much money you have. And it's pretty hard to plan for retirement if you don't know how much money you have.

So, how do you solve the inherent tax problems associated with owning an annuity inside an IRA? You have to have an annuity that has what I describe as a **Piecemeal Internal Roth Conversion**. This feature allows you to shift money from your IRA annuity to a Roth IRA annuity in whatever amount you want over whatever time frame your financial plan calls for. Once you complete that Roth conversion, you can begin drawing guaranteed lifetime income that's tax-free. Furthermore, because distributions from Roth IRAs don't count as Provisional Income,[7] this increases the likelihood you'll receive your Social Security 100% tax-free.

So, what do we make of this claim? Mostly *false*.

Next, Ken Fisher talks about the annuity's perceived illiquidity.

Criticism #4: "Annuities are hard to get out of once you're in them."

Here, Fisher is referring to the annuity's surrender charges. Do annuities have surrender charges? They sure do. But, if you have a guarantee that you'll never run out of money so long as you're alive, why would you surrender your annuity?

So, how do we judge this claim? *Simplistic*. The reality is that the decision of whether or not to incorporate annuities into your retirement plan is much more nuanced than Fisher lets on.

Next, Ken Fisher weighs in on the physical size of the annuity contract.

---

7. Provisional Income is the income the IRS tracks to determine if they are going to tax your Social Security. 1099s from your taxable investments, distributions from your tax-deferred investments, interest from municipal bonds, and one-half of your Social Security all count as Provisional Income.

Criticism #5: "Annuities are extremely confusing, with a contract that's about an inch thick."

More hyperbole on the part of Ken Fisher. The fact is, I've seen hundreds of annuity contracts and the vast majority are thinner than most prospectuses you would ever receive from Fisher Investments.

Now, do these contracts use legalese to describe the guarantees that annuities provide? You would certainly hope so. If what you're looking for is guaranteed income for life, you want those guarantees described in iron-clad, rock-solid legal terms that you can count on, rain or shine. And yes, those guarantees are found in the annuity contract.

So, how do we characterize this claim? *Wrong*.

Next, Ken Fisher claims that annuities are not designed to provide the investor any real benefit.

Criticism #6: "These products are not made to benefit the customer."

The whole purpose of an annuity is to provide you a benefit that literally can't be provided in any other way. The goal here is to guarantee your living expenses regardless of what's happening in the stock market or on the geopolitical scene and regardless of how long you live.

Furthermore, there's a long list of health and psychological benefits associated with guaranteed lifetime income that you almost certainly won't get through a Fisher Investments portfolio. We're talking more predictability in retirement, less anxiety, and according to Stephen Dubner of Freakonomics, a longer life. Dubner says, "It's that little extra incentive of the annuity payout that keeps people going."

What's more, if you have your basic living expenses guaranteed in retirement, you now have the luxury of taking more risk with your stock market investments. Even if your portfolio goes down as a result of that increased risk, you now have the flexibility to watch it recover before taking further distributions. And this increases the likelihood that your investments will last through life expectancy.

So, what do we make of this claim? Ken Fisher is actually *180 degrees wrong*. In fact, if he were any more wrong on this, he'd be veering his way back toward right again!

Criticism #7: "The real winner is the salesperson."

This is coming from the guy who is currently worth $7.1 billion. Now, there's nothing inherently wrong with being worth $7.1 billion, but it's clear that he built that kind of wealth by providing a service with a perceived benefit. So, when you roll your money over to Fisher Investments, I think we can all agree that Ken Fisher is one of the huge winners in that transaction. Do financial advisors who recommend annuities get paid for their recommendations? Certainly, but it's disingenuous at best for a billionaire who has profited enormously over the years from making financial recommendations to criticize a financial advisor for getting compensated for recommending a financial tool that guarantees the retiree will never run out of money.

So, how would I characterize this claim? *Disingenuous.*

Lastly, Ken Fisher says there are better ways to do what an annuity claims to be able to do.

Criticism #8: "Anything you want to do with annuities, there's a better way to do."

What Fisher is referring to here is, of course, the Four Percent Rule. He maintains it's the "better way" to purge longevity risk from your retirement picture, notwithstanding its manifold shortcomings. As I've already shown, a guaranteed lifetime income annuity can neutralize longevity risk far more effectively and for much less money than Ken Fisher's stock market approach.

If anything, Ken Fisher is consistent. Consistently wrong. His criticisms against annuities often come across as simplistic and dangerously short-sighted.

SUMMARY

There are two ways to purge longevity risk from your retirement outlook. The first is endorsed by nearly every mainstream guru and is referred to as the stock market approach. Accumulate a huge pile of money and then constrain yourself to a 4% distribution rate over the arc of your retirement. The success of this approach is contingent upon suppressing a variety of investor behaviors that dramatically erode returns over time. Furthermore, it requires you to accumulate a massive pile of money by day-1 of retirement. And if you aren't on track, you'll have to save more, spend less, work longer, die sooner, or take more risk in the stock market to bridge that retirement shortfall.

The second approach to mitigating longevity risk is the guaranteed lifetime income approach in the form of an annuity. This time-tested financial tool is sharply condemned by every financial guru we've thus far discussed, the most prominent of whom is Ken Fisher. Notwithstanding the hate campaign they've long waged against this financial tool, annuities can help you neutralize longevity risk, and the subset of risks it amplifies, less expensively and more effectively than the guru-endorsed stock market approach.

3
Solving Tax Rate Risk

When I published *The Power of Zero* in 2014, I argued that our nation's massively unfunded obligations for Social Security, Medicare, and Medicaid would force the federal government to raise taxes to stratospheric levels or risk going broke. I drew upon the testimony of former comptroller general of the federal government David M. Walker, who predicted that tax rates would have to double by 2030 or the United States would have to impose dramatic, across-the-board cuts to our nation's entitlement programs.

I have since become acquainted with the work of Dr. Larry Kotlikoff of Boston University, who is the foremost expert in the world on what has come to be known as *Fiscal Gap Accounting*. According to Kotlikoff, the way our federal government quantifies the national debt is not only wrong and misleading but at odds with how every other developed nation in the world does it. To paint a more accurate picture, Dr. Kotlikoff projects out over the next 75 years everything the federal government has promised to pay for Social Security, Medicare, Medicaid, interest on the national debt, and the general cost of running the federal government. He then projects out over that same time frame the amount of money the US Treasury plans to bring in under current tax rates. If there's a difference between those two numbers, Kotlikoff explains, then your country has a fiscal gap. And that's its true national debt. Our nation's actual debt isn't $34 trillion (as it was at the time of this writing), as the federal government would have you believe. It's actually much closer to $239 trillion.[1] Put differently, we would have to have $239 trillion sitting in a bank account today earning Treasury rates (about 5%) to deliver on everything that we've promised that we can't afford to pay.

Back in 2014, I received a lot of online criticism for making the claim that tax rates would have to go higher in the future to keep our country solvent. Tax rates, these keyboard warriors insisted, tended to ebb and flow over time, so it was useless to build a retirement strategy around what you *anticipated* tax rates might be in the future. What they seemed to be saying was that the fiscal condition of our country at that time was no different than at any other point in our history and there was little cause for alarm.

However, an interesting thing has happened since

---

1. "Kotlikoff: Real Federal Debt Is $239 Trillion," Goodman Institute, December 3, 2019, https://www.goodmaninstitute.org/2019/12/03/kotlikoff-real-federal-debt-is-239-trillion/.

those critics raised their objections in 2014. As the fiscal trajectory of our country has grown more and more unsustainable with the passing of time, the financial gurus we've discussed thus far have come out overwhelmingly in favor of tax-free investment accounts. Dave Ramsey's website, for example, fully endorses Roth IRAs and Roth 401(k)s over IRAs and traditional 401(k)s. Suze Orman likewise endorses Roth accounts because she anticipates that tax rates will "skyrocket" in the coming years.[2]

SO, WHAT'S THE PROBLEM?

This is great news! you must be thinking. While most gurus haven't historically been on the cutting edge of tax-free retirement strategies, they *have* eventually come around, and they should be commended for their proactivity, right? While I do congratulate them for their willingness to go against convention when it comes to the types of retirement accounts they recommend, one huge problem remains. These gurus *have* embraced tax-free investment strategies, but they continue to succumb

---

2. "How to Save for Retirement: Suze Orman Shares Her Best Money Advice," TODAY, March 18, 2019, https://www.youtube.com/watch?v=TS4EeLZ4M70.

to all the same age-old, guru-centric problems I high-lighted in chapter 1. Their strategies and recommendations are still far too broad, generalized, and devoid of nuance to be useful to the disciplined, sophisticated investor. They pay lip service to the idea of a tax-free retirement but they give personalized, detailed tax-free strategy short shrift. In fact, in some cases, their advice can be reckless and costly.

In this chapter I will compare the gurus' tax-free recommendations with the detailed, specific, math-based Power of Zero strategies that I've developed over the last 20 years. By the end of this chapter, you'll be armed with all the strategy you'll need to shield your hard-earned retirement savings from the impact of dramatically higher taxes.

THE MEASURING STICK OF A SOLID ROTH CONVERSION STRATEGY

The single greatest way to shield your existing retirement savings from higher taxes is the Roth conversion. But as you shall soon see, not all Roth conversion advice is created equal. A Roth conversion strategy must answer three basic questions if it's going to effectively shield your retirement savings from the impact of higher taxes. These questions are as follows:

1. What overall amount should be converted?
2. What should the size of each annual conversion be?
3. What is the time frame over which the conversion should be completed?

Let's begin by answering each one of these questions from a Power of Zero perspective.

1. What Overall Amount Should Be Converted?

Let's say you have $1,000,000 in your IRA[3] and you're absolutely convinced that tax rates in the future are likely to be dramatically higher than they are today. How much of that million dollars should be converted to Roth? Some? Most? All? If we're leaving some or most in the tax-deferred bucket, what's our justification for doing so?

To understand the total amount of your IRA that

---

3. While I refer to IRAs in this chapter, I could just as easily be referring to 401(k)s, 403(b)s, SEPs, SIMPLEs, etc., as they are all taxed in the same way.

shield your retirement savings from the impact of higher taxes. These questions are as follows:

1. What overall amount should be converted?
2. What should the size of each annual conversion be?
3. What is the time frame over which the conversion should be completed?

Let's begin by answering each one of these questions from a Power of Zero perspective.

1. What Overall Amount Should Be Converted?

Let's say you have $1,000,000 in your IRA[3] and you're absolutely convinced that tax rates in the future are likely to be dramatically higher than they are today. How much of that million dollars should be converted to Roth? Some? Most? All? If we're leaving some or most in the tax-deferred bucket, what's our justification for doing so?

To understand the total amount of your IRA that

---

3. While I refer to IRAs in this chapter, I could just as easily be referring to 401(k)s, 403(b)s, SEPs, SIMPLEs, etc., as they are all taxed in the same way.

to all the same age-old, guru-centric problems I highlighted in chapter 1. Their strategies and recommendations are still far too broad, generalized, and devoid of nuance to be useful to the disciplined, sophisticated investor. They pay lip service to the idea of a tax-free retirement but they give personalized, detailed tax-free strategy short shrift. In fact, in some cases, their advice can be reckless and costly.

In this chapter I will compare the gurus' tax-free recommendations with the detailed, specific, math-based Power of Zero strategies that I've developed over the last 20 years. By the end of this chapter, you'll be armed with all the strategy you'll need to shield your hard-earned retirement savings from the impact of dramatically higher taxes.

THE MEASURING STICK OF A SOLID ROTH CONVERSION STRATEGY

The single greatest way to shield your existing retirement savings from higher taxes is the Roth conversion. But as you shall soon see, not all Roth conversion advice is created equal. A Roth conversion strategy must answer three basic questions if it's going to effectively

However, let's say that you're currently in the 22% tax bracket, and I recommend a strategy that bumps you up into the 24% tax bracket. I did so, by the way, because, for an additional 2%, you can convert an extra $182,850 per year and dramatically increase the likelihood of converting that $1,000,000 to Roth before tax rates go up for good. How do you think this recommendation would go down? Rather easily, I'd venture to say. In an effort to avoid a doubling of tax rates over time, we increased your tax bracket ever so slightly, on the margin. By a measly 2%.

3. What Is the Time Frame Over Which the Conversion Should Be Completed?

The time frame over which you should complete your conversion is inextricably connected to the size of each annual conversion. Roth conversions should not be open-ended strategies. You shouldn't be thinking, *Let's start today and just see how things go!* You should determine how much of your tax-deferred assets need to be converted, the amount of tax you're comfortable paying, and ultimately the end date by which the conversion should be executed. This end date should be a point in time before which you think tax rates are likely to rise dramatically. For example, if you think taxes are going to skyrocket in 2031, complete your Roth conversion in or before 2030.

Beware the 32% Tax Bracket

You should generally avoid a Roth conversion strategy that bumps you into the 32% tax bracket (the next highest above 24%). This guideline can help clarify the time frame over which you should execute your Roth conversion. For example, let's say you're married and filing jointly, your taxable income is $100,000 (putting you squarely in the 22% tax bracket), and the top of the 24% tax bracket is $383,900. That means you could convert $283,900 per year without bumping into the 32% tax bracket. If you wanted to convert $1,000,000 to a Roth, you could easily do so over the next four years. Now, keep in mind that this four-year conversion *will* extend beyond December 31, 2025, when tax rates revert back to what they were in 2017. And even though that 24% bracket would rise to 28% in 2026, you'll still be paying less than 32%.

When Is the Drop-Dead Date for Completing Your Roth Conversion Strategy?

All this said, *is* there a deadline by which you should complete your Roth conversion strategy? Is there a point in time when our country's financial chickens come home to roost and the government is forced to raise tax rates? The answer is a resounding yes. There will come a time when interest on the national debt begins to crowd out major budget items like Social Security, Medicare, and Medicaid and the government will be forced to raise taxes. What's worse, Medicare will no longer be able to pay all its bills in 2036. And, if Congress doesn't dramatically restructure Social Security, recipients will see across-the-board cuts of 23% starting in 2034. Given the federal government's penchant for procrastination, I foresee them kicking the can down the road until 2030 or so before being forced to raise taxes. That means that you have a seven- or eight-year period (at the time of this writing) within which to fully execute your Roth conversion strategy. And every year that goes by where you fail to take advantage of historically low tax rates is potentially a year beyond 2030 in which you could be forced to pay the highest tax rates you're likely to see in your lifetime.

4. Bonus Requirement: Factual Accuracy

Beyond answering the three basic questions I mention above, a good Roth conversion strategy should be technically accurate. The rules around Roth conversions can be tricky and need to be navigated with a deft hand. Given this complexity, it isn't hard to see how a one-size-fits-all financial guru could easily lead their followers astray.

EVALUATING DAVE RAMSEY'S ROTH CONVERSION ADVICE

Now that we know the three basic components of an effective Roth conversion strategy, we have a framework within which to evaluate the Roth conversion advice dispensed by the most famous financial guru of them all, Dave Ramsey. Remember, my aim is not to intentionally malign, but to advance the dialogue around proven, math-based retirement strategies that shield you from the impact of higher taxes and maximize your after-tax cash flow in retirement.

Alright, let's dive in. Given Ramsey's embrace of the tax-free paradigm, it isn't surprising that his website is overflowing with articles on how to execute a Roth conversion. But as you will soon see, when it comes to Roth conversion advice, he values quantity far more than he does specificity and accuracy.

In an article on Ramsey's website, I was encouraged by how things started out:

> *Well, given today's reduced individual tax rates, you may wind up in a higher tax bracket in retirement. So, paying the taxes up front for a Roth conversion— if you can afford it—and getting the money out tax-free in retirement, is one of those times when paying a little now can save you a bundle later.*[4]

Good job, Dave. This is a perfectly adequate summation of why Roth conversions make sense. Your tax rate in retirement could end up being higher than it is today. I would have liked a few more details on why individual tax rates could go up, and perhaps how high, but it was a good start, nonetheless.

---

4. "What Is a Roth Conversion?," Ramsey Solutions, September 27, 2021, https://www.ramseysolutions.com/retirement/what-is-a-roth -conversion.

As Ramsey continues, he indirectly addresses one of the three components of a good Roth conversion strategy: how much you should convert in a year. He does so by warning that a Roth conversion could bump you into a higher tax bracket.

Let's talk about tax rates first. Because the conversion amount is added to your taxable income, it could potentially bump up your tax bracket.

After reading this warning, I was fully prepared for him to discuss the dangers of a Roth conversion strategy that bumps you from 12% to 22%. Again, in the name of protecting yourself against higher tax rates in the future, you'd be doubling your taxes today. You should avoid that approach at all costs. I was not prepared for what Ramsey said next:

So, for example, a married couple filing jointly in 2020 with a taxable income of $100,000 pays 22% in taxes and can convert up to $71,050 without hitting the next tax bracket, which begins at $171,051 and is taxed at 24%. Now, paying the taxes on this conversion would break down like this: Let's say you have $100,000 in a traditional 401(k), and you want to convert it to a Roth IRA.

You'll pay 22% on the first $71,050 ($15,631 in taxes), and 24% on the remaining $28,950 ($6,948 in taxes) for a total tax hit of $22,579 on the conversion.[5]

Okay, Dave Ramsey is to be commended for warning us that Roth conversions could bump you into a higher tax bracket. But, amazingly, he uses the 24% tax bracket to illustrate the consequences of doing so. Instead of talking about the 24% bracket as an opportunity of historical proportions, as the sweet spot in the Trump tax cuts, he makes it the poster child for Roth conversion overexuberance.

Look, if you're okay with the 22% tax bracket, why wouldn't you take full advantage of the 24% bracket as well? Again, for only 2% more, it allows you to convert another $182,850 to your tax-free bucket. In fact, if you have $1,000,000 or more in your IRA, you'll never convert it all to Roth before tax rates go up for good *without* taking advantage of the 24% bracket. So, no, the 24% tax bracket is not a liability or a penalty for overzealous Roth converters. Rather, it's a massive sweet spot in what I frequently refer to as the tax sale of a lifetime.

---

5. Ibid.

Next, Ramsey asks you to consider how you're planning to pay taxes on your Roth conversion.

And you want to seriously consider doing a Roth conversion only if *you can afford to pay the tax bill with cash. No exceptions, guys! A conversion could add* thousands *of dollars to your tax bill.*[6]

Okay, did Ramsey *really* just say that? Do you know how many people I come across day in and day out who have enough liquid cash to pay the tax on their Roth conversion? Maybe like 5%. It's more like, they have $1,000,000 in their IRA, and have just enough cash in their savings account to pass for an emergency fund. Hardly sufficient to pay the tax on their entire Roth conversion. In other words, if everyone followed Ramsey's advice, only one in twenty investors would consider Roth conversions.

Let me see if I can cast Ramsey's advice in a slightly different light. Your IRA is sitting on the tracks with a massive tax freight train bearing down on it, and you should only consider a Roth conversion if you have the cash with which to pay the tax? And if you don't have

---

6. Ibid.

the cash, you must sit there and watch helplessly as that tax freight train destroys your retirement savings?

Now, let me be clear—there are two instances where you will *have* to use cash to pay the taxes on your Roth conversion: when you're younger than 59½ and when you're doing a Roth 401(k) conversion. Both scenarios *require* you to use cash to pay the tax on your conversion. But Ramsey doesn't make this distinction. So, you're simply left to conclude that the only time you should ever do a Roth conversion is if you have cash on hand with which to pay the tax.

Folks, if you don't have cash to pay the tax, *there is no harm in having the IRS withhold the tax from the Roth conversion itself,* so long as you're older than 59½ and it's not a Roth 401(k) conversion. It's not optimal, but it's far better than the alternative, which is to simply leave the money in your IRA and watch helplessly as tax rates double over time. Most Americans will eventually pay taxes out of their IRA distributions in retirement (it's called withholding), so what's the harm in paying taxes on your conversion out of the IRA itself? Furthermore, if you pay those taxes now, you'll be doing so at historically low tax rates, and if you're over age 59½, there are no penalties for doing so.

Beware of the Five-Year Rule!

Unfortunately, Ramsey's ill-advised prescriptions for Roth conversions don't stop here. Let's keep reading:

> When it comes to Roth conversions, it could be the right call for you if your timeline to retirement is more than five years. The money you convert into a Roth IRA must *stay there for a five-year period. If you withdraw money before the five-year period, you may pay a 10% penalty and additional income taxes.*[7]

Here, Ramsey identifies the five-year Roth conversion rule that says that you may pay a 10% penalty and additional income taxes if you access your converted dollars inside a five-year window. But here's the problem: the 10% penalty and additional taxes during the five-year waiting period only apply to those who are younger than 59½ as a way of preventing them from simply converting their IRA to Roth and then accessing the money.[8] What Ramsey doesn't tell you is that

---

7. Ibid.

8. Growth on any Roth converted amounts can be accessed tax-free post 59½ so long as five years have passed since the first Roth contribution *or* Roth conversion.

if you're over age 59½, the 10% penalty won't apply to you. It only applies to people who are *younger* than 59½!

The other thing that bothers me about this particular piece of advice is, if you take Ramsey at his word, you shouldn't consider a Roth conversion unless you're more than five years from retirement. Strangely, he's using the five-year holding rule as the reason for avoiding the Roth conversion altogether. It's like saying, "You shouldn't have spaghetti for lunch because it's raining outside!" The one has absolutely no bearing on the other.

Here's an example to illustrate the danger of this advice, particularly in a rising tax rate environment. Let's say that you just retired at age 60 and are considering a Roth conversion. According to the Ramsey Rule, the Roth conversion is off the table. Why? Because you're within five years of retirement! Never mind that you may be in a lower tax bracket in retirement than you were during your working years. Never mind that you're convinced that tax rates even 10 years from now are likely to be dramatically higher than they are today. No soup for you! Because you violated Ramsey's squirrelly application of the five-year holding rule, you can no longer shield your retirement savings from the impact of higher taxes! Too bad, so sad!

Summary

Not only does Ramsey's Roth conversion doctrine not address the three basic components of a sound Roth conversion strategy, but he fails to consider a crucial aspect in Trump's tax cuts. First, he doesn't understand that the 24% bracket is the sweet spot in the Trump tax cuts and should figure prominently in your Roth conversion strategy, particularly if you have a large balance in your IRA. Second, he insists that you should only do a Roth conversion if you have cash on hand with which to pay the tax. And finally, he says you should only consider a Roth conversion if you're five years or more from retirement.

Why does Ramsey make such disastrously wrong prescriptions when it comes to tax-free retirement strategies? Again, he never had a chance to marinate in time-tested, math-based financial principles, so he doesn't have a technically accurate understanding of Roth conversion rules. Moreover, because he's addressing a widely diverse audience, he has to create one-size-fits-all axioms that are pithy and memorable, but that ultimately lead his listeners astray. As a result, his followers may end up paying hundreds of thousands of dollars in unnecessary taxes at a period in their lives when they can least afford to do so: in retirement.

CONCLUSION

Maximizing your after-tax income in retirement often involves complex strategy, particularly when it involves a Roth conversion. You have to accurately calculate the amount of your overall conversion, the annual conversion amounts, and the time frame over which the conversion should be completed. If you take your financial cues from mainstream gurus such as Dave Ramsey, however, you'll have to wade through vague explanations, one-size-fits-all axioms, and factual inaccuracies that could derail your tax-free retirement strategy altogether. And, unfortunately, when it comes to making decisions on the timing and amounts of tax payments on your retirement savings, you only have one chance to get it right.

4

Verboten: Cash Value Life Insurance

I f there's one thing that financial gurus universally agree upon, it's that there is almost never a scenario in which you should incorporate cash value life insurance into your retirement plan. We're talking Whole Life, Variable Universal Life, Indexed Universal Life, Universal Life, you name it. If your life insurance policy doesn't begin with the word *term*, then you'd just as soon throw an albatross around your financial neck and toss yourself into the sea. That's how pernicious and destructive it can be to your long-term financial outlook, or so the gurus say.

A BLACK-AND-WHITE APPROACH

Never has the black-and-white, one-size-fits-all approach to retirement planning been more on full display than when it comes to cash value life insurance. Don't believe me? Well, here's a small sampling of what our favorite gurus have said.

Suze Orman

When it comes to cash value life insurance, Orman's position is clear and unequivocal.

Please listen to me: life insurance is an expensive way to invest. Anyone who is trying to sell you life insurance as an investment is not acting in your best interest.

And:

Whenever someone tries to sell you a life insurance policy with some story that it is a fantastic way to invest, you are to shut down that conversation and never work with that person again.[1]

Okay, so life insurance should never be integrated into your retirement plan *and*, if a financial advisor so much as brings it up, you are to sever the relationship immediately.

Dave Ramsey

Ramsey is no less vociferous when it comes to the evils of permanent life insurance. He says:

Permanent life insurance . . . might sound like a

---

1. "Is Life Insurance a Good Investment?," Suze Orman, n.d., https://www.suzeorman.com/blog/Is-Life-Insurance-a-Good-Investment.

good deal. But trust us, it's hot garbage. All forms
of whole life insurance [Ramsey uses Whole Life
as a catchall phrase to describe every variety
of cash value life insurance] *try to combine two*
goals (life insurance and savings) into one prod-
uct. The thing is, it doesn't do either very well. It's
way more expensive than term life insurance, and
the savings side of whole life policies almost always
sucks because you end up paying so many fees.[2]

In summary, all cash value life insurance is hot garbage because of its high fees and, in the end, does a
horrible job at both the savings and the protection components of what it's designed to do.

Ramit Sethi

The host of Netflix's *How to Get Rich* wrote a bestselling
book back in 2009 entitled *I Will Teach You to Be Rich*
in which he discusses how a friend got ripped off by a
"financial advisor." Here's what he had to say:

---

2. George Kamel, "What Is Life Insurance?," Ramsey Solutions,
May 20, 2024, https://www.ramseysolutions.com/insurance/what
-is-life-insurance.

Years ago, my friend Joe emailed me asking me to take a look at his investments. He suspected he was being taken for a ride by his financial advisor. Within five minutes of talking to him, I knew he was in a bad situation. Joe is a young entrepreneur with high earnings, so this advisor figured he was a meal ticket for the next four decades.

I told him the following, "There are certain keywords that are major red flags when it comes to investing, including 'whole life insurance,' 'annuities,' and 'primerica.' Any of those words means, at best, you're almost certainly overpaying and at worst, you're being scammed."

Here, Sethi doesn't provide any solid evidence for why he considers permanent life insurance (or annuities, for that matter) a scam. Like his mainstream financial guru cohorts, he blithely dismisses it with a simple wave of the hand.

Clark Howard

Clark Howard is no less vocal when it comes to decrying the dangers of permanent life insurance. According to his website,

Most life insurance options outside of term life are garbage. They serve to line the pockets of the insurance agent through high commissions and fees. That includes whole life insurance.[3]

Once again, we see the words *garbage* and *life insurance* in the same sentence. Are you starting to detect a pattern?

THANKS FOR BEARING WITH ME

Okay, I appreciate you wading through all that permanent life insurance invective to start out the chapter. My goal was to simply demonstrate that there is near universal agreement among mainstream financial gurus that permanent life insurance should not only be excluded from your retirement plan, but that it's a steaming hot pile of garbage peddled by avaricious life insurance agents whose sole goal is to line their pockets with sky-high commissions.

Now that I've laid out the guru consensus on the

---

3. Christopher Smith, "4 Insurance Policies You Actually Need (and 6 You Don't)," Clark Howard, August 19, 2022, https://clark .com/insurance/insurance-policies-you-need/.

horrors of cash value life insurance, let's use a little math to debunk their claims once and for all. Throughout this chapter I will explore several contexts in which cash value life insurance not only is *not* a steaming hot pile of garbage, but can actually extend the life of your investments and mitigate a number of insidious risks that can send your retirement plan cartwheeling off the tracks.

APPLICATION #1: THE VOLATILITY SHIELD

The first context in which permanent life insurance can enhance your retirement picture is when it's used as what I refer to as a *Volatility Shield*.

To explain how a Volatility Shield works and why you might need one, let's briefly revisit the Four Percent Rule. As a reminder, it states that if you want a reasonably high likelihood that your money will last through life expectancy, you should never withdraw more than 4% of your day-1 retirement balance per year, adjusted every year thereafter for inflation. As I explained in chapter 2, there's a glaring problem with the Four Percent Rule. It's a pretty expensive way to go about saving for retirement. For example, if you need

$100,000 to meet your annual retirement needs, and the most you can ever take out is 4%, adjusted every year thereafter for inflation, you will have to accumulate $2,500,000 by the time you retire.

If you aren't on track to accumulate the required amount by retirement, you'll need to resort to those five unsavory alternatives I mentioned earlier: save more, spend less, work longer, die sooner, or take more risks in the stock market. Let's examine each of these unsavory alternatives a little more in depth.

1. Save More

This means trimming back your lifestyle during your working years so you can contribute more to your retirement plan.

2. Spend Less

This involves lowering your lifestyle expectations in retirement. Planning on living on $100,000 per year? Think again. To make your money last, you might just have to downgrade to $80,000 per year or less.

3. Work Longer

Planning on retiring at 65? Well, how about pushing

that out to age 70 to give your retirement savings a little more time to grow and compound? As an added "bonus," this would shorten the time period over which your retirement savings would be required to last.

4. Die Sooner

This recommendation is entirely tongue in cheek. However, it is true that people with shorter life expectancies don't have to save as much money because their retirement savings aren't required to last as long.

5. Take More Risk in the Stock Market

Instead of adopting the traditional 60/40 stock-bond mix, you'll need to allocate a greater share of your assets to the stock market in the hopes of increasing your return over time. Of course, taking more market risk is no guarantee, either, and you could end up missing your retirement goal by an even wider margin.

The Sixth Way

What if I told you there was a sixth option, entirely ignored by mainstream financial gurus, that could help you bridge your retirement shortfall without all the angst that goes along with the five above-mentioned approaches? Option number six is an alternative I refer to as the Volatility Shield.

Before I delve into the details of the Volatility Shield, let's lay a little foundation. As it turns out, the reason you can only withdraw 4% of your stock market portfolio per year is because, in the first 10 years of retirement, you're likely to experience two to three down years in the market. If you retire at the wrong time in history, it could be as many as four or five. When you withdraw money to pay for your lifestyle needs in the years following a market loss, it deals a serious blow to the statistical likelihood of your retirement savings lasting through your actuarial life expectancy. It's sort of like kicking your retirement savings while they're down. If you cap your withdrawals at 4% per year, however, your portfolio has a much higher likelihood of weathering a withdrawal and a market loss within the same year.

But what if there were a way to avoid having to take money out of your stock market portfolio following the down years in that first decade of retirement? What if you could pay for your living expenses out of your Volatility Shield, giving your retirement savings a chance to recover before you took further distributions? According to Monte Carlo simulations, you could increase your sustainable withdrawal rate in retirement to as high as 8% with a sky-high likelihood that your money would last through life expectancy.

The Proof Is in the Pudding

In the following chart, I show the likelihood that your retirement savings would last through life expectancy if you took 8% withdrawal rates and incorporated a Volatility Shield into your income plan. Note that the more living expenses you accumulate in your Volatility Shield, the higher the likelihood your stock market savings will last through life expectancy.

YEARS OF LIVING EXPENSES ACCUMULATED	SUCCESS RATE OVER 30-YEAR RETIREMENT
1	77%
2	82%
3	86%
4	90%
5	93%
6	96%

As you can see, if you can accumulate five years' worth of living expenses in your Volatility Shield by day-1 of retirement, you can take 8% annual withdrawals from your stock market portfolio with a 93% likelihood that your money will last for a full 30-year retirement! Contrast that with Dave Ramsey's 8% withdrawal rate that has an anemic 37% success rate. There's no comparison!

Required Attributes of a Volatility Shield

Before I reveal the identity of the Volatility Shield, let's discuss all the attributes it must possess.

1. Safe and Productive Growth

First, the Volatility Shield must grow safely and productively. You can't combat market risk with an account that's *exposed* to market risk. I'm looking for an account with a rock-solid guarantee against market loss. Second, we need to get reasonable rates of return over time. I'm talking between 5% and 7% net of fees over the life of the program. It will be much easier to accumulate the amount of capital required to shield yourself from volatility in retirement if that money is growing productively between now and then.

2. Tax-Free

Next, this account must grow tax-free *and* allow for tax-free distributions. By combining these attributes, your money will grow more efficiently, and you won't have to allocate as much money to the account along the way. Further, when you have the luxury of taking tax-free distributions, you aren't exposed to increases in tax rates over time. You won't be in a position where a dramatic rise in tax rates will crater your spending power in retirement.

And lastly, if those distributions are truly tax-free, they won't count as Provisional Income. That means they won't count against the thresholds that cause Social Security taxation. And if you don't have to compensate for taxes on your Social Security, your money lasts longer.

3. Fully Funded by Day-1 of Retirement

Lastly, your Volatility Shield must be *fully funded* and raring to go by day-1 of retirement. That means you'll need to have saved at least three years' worth of living expenses. Why is this so important? Because you never know when the stock market is going to tank. If you retire during a down market, you must be prepared to immediately take distributions from your Volatility Shield to cover lifestyle expenses. This will give your portfolio a chance to recover before you take further withdrawals.

The Volatility Shield Revealed

Right about now you may be thinking, *We really have to align the stars on this one, Dave! We're talking a blue moon on a Wednesday. You're asking for safe and productive growth along with tax-free accumulation and tax-free distributions?! Not going to happen!*

The truth is, an account with precisely these attributes actually does exist, and it's been right under your nose all along. The only account that satisfies every single one of the above-mentioned requirements is cash value life insurance. Hmm. Maybe 100% of cash value life insurance *doesn't* suck 100% of the time!

After studying the qualities of various types of cash value life insurance over the last 25 years, I have concluded that the policy most ideally suited to the Volatility Shield concept is *Indexed Universal Life* (*IUL*).

Why Is Indexed Universal Life the Ideal Volatility Shield?

When it comes to the ideal Volatility Shield, the IUL is the only alternative that has *all* of the attributes you'll need to protect your retirement savings from volatility during those critical first 10 years in retirement.

Safe and Productive

When structured properly and through the right carrier, the IUL has proven, historical returns of between 5% and 7% net of fees over time. All this without taking any more market risk than what you're accustomed to taking in your savings account!

Tax-Free and Cost-Free

All cash value life insurance policies allow you take money out tax-free by way of a policy loan. But here's the catch: most companies charge you a net rate of interest to access those funds. And if you don't pay this interest back at the end of the year, they'll subtract it from your cash value. As you continue to take future loans, your interest will grow and compound to the point where it could bankrupt your policy. Not only would you lose your death benefit, but you'd receive a massive tax bill from the IRS for your trouble. Not so if you utilize an IUL through the right carrier. In fact, several life insurance companies *guarantee* that your IUL distributions are both tax-free and cost-free. This way you're never in a position where snowballing interest threatens to bankrupt your policy.

Aligning the Stars

Because the IUL grows safely and productively *and* allows for tax-free growth, you run a much higher likelihood of accumulating the required amount by day-1 of retirement. Moreover, because IULs through certain carriers allow for tax-free *and* cost-free distributions, you can shield yourself from the impact of higher taxes and the effects of compounding interest. In my chapter 5 case study, I'll show you how mathematically impactful a Volatility Shield can be on a real-life retirement plan.

How Quickly Can I Fund My Volatility Shield?

Because of the IRS rules that govern the funding of Indexed Universal Life policies, you can't fully fund your Volatility Shield overnight. You'll need to make contributions for at least five years, and then let that money marinate another five years before you take distributions. So, if you're planning on retiring at age 65, you should probably start funding your Volatility Shield by the time you're 55.

Why Can't I Fund My Volatility Shield in Retirement?

If you don't begin to fund your IUL until you're retired, you'll be facing two rather significant challenges. First, in order for the Volatility Shield concept to work, it must be in place by day-1 of retirement. Remember, you never know when a down year in the market is likely to befall you. It could well happen in the very year you retire. Second, because it takes at least 10 years for your Volatility Shield to fully mature, you'll be well past the first decade of retirement (the real danger zone) by the time you're ready to take those tax-free distributions. That's well beyond the period in your retirement where the Volatility Shield can make the most impact.

A Silver Lining

If you're already retired, there is a slight variation on the Volatility Shield concept that doesn't have the same incubation period as Indexed Universal Life, and that's the guaranteed lifetime income annuity we discussed in chapter 2. Because your guaranteed lifetime income annuity pays for your lifestyle needs in retirement, rain or shine, it can give the stock market portion of your portfolio a chance to recover before you take further distributions.

Rule of Thumb

In short, if you're at least 10 years away from retirement, you have plenty of time to fully fund your Indexed Universal Life insurance policy and utilize it as a viable Volatility Shield. If you're within 10 years of retirement, the guaranteed lifetime income annuity has similar attributes that can likewise shield you from the effects of market volatility. As I demonstrate in chapter 6, however, you're much better off if you incorporate *both* financial tools into your retirement plan.

Ernst & Young Weighs In

While I have done hundreds of thousands of my own Monte Carlo simulations to corroborate the math and science behind the Volatility Shield concept, it's encouraging to know that there are third-party organizations that have likewise put it under the microscope. One such company is the world-renowned CPA firm Ernst & Young. In a recent study, they touted the benefits of using cash value life insurance as a Volatility Shield in retirement.[4] In their study, they demonstrated how investors who earmark 30% of their retirement savings toward cash value life insurance can take superior levels of income from their stock market portfolios in retirement over those who take a strict stock market–only approach. How is this possible? Once again, when you pay for your living expenses from your life insurance cash value in the years following a

---

4. Justin Singer, "How Life Insurers Can Provide Differentiated Retirement Benefits," n.d., https://www.ey.com/en_us/insurance /how-life-insurers-can-provide-differentiated-retirement-benefits.

down year in the stock market, you give your investment portfolio a chance to recover before taking further distributions. And this dramatically increases the amount of sustainable income you can distribute from your portfolio over the arc of a full 30-year retirement.

Summary

If you aren't on track to reach your retirement goals by day-1 of retirement, you must resort to an array of angst-inducing alternatives that are enough to make you want to throw in the towel altogether. The standard fixes involve saving more, spending less, working longer, dying sooner, or taking more risk in the stock market. By availing yourself of a sixth option—what I refer to as a Volatility Shield—you can bridge your retirement shortfall without all the heartburn associated with the traditional approaches. By using your Volatility Shield to pay for living expenses in the year following a down year in the market, you give your retirement portfolio a chance to recover before taking further withdrawals. This alone can increase your sustainable distribution rate in retirement to as high as 8% per year, while dramatically increasing the likelihood that your stock market savings will last through life expectancy. The cash value life insurance policy that makes for the most efficient and effective Volatility Shield is Indexed Universal Life. It's the only one that combines safe and productive growth along with tax-free *and* cost-free distributions.

APPLICATION #2: LONG-TERM CARE

The second context in which cash value makes sense is as a means of mitigating the risk of long-term care. First, let's lay a little groundwork. A long-term care event may well be the single most devastating thing that could befall you in retirement (financially speaking, of course). Here's why. Before the government lifts a finger to help, you'll be forced to spend down most of your retirement savings. So, what was shaping up to be a perfectly rosy retirement for the community spouse[5] turns into basic, bare-bones, subsistence-type living. I broach the topic of long-term care with just about everyone who steps foot in my office for two very important reasons:

---

5. Community spouse: the husband or wife of a long-term care recipient.

1. **The Likelihood of a Long-Term Care Event:** The most recent statistics show that there's a 70% chance that at least one spouse will suffer a health event that requires long-term care.

2. **The Costs of a Long-Term Care Event:** The expense of a long-term care event can, in a very short period of time, destroy a lifetime of savings, leaving the community spouse financially devastated.

These facts are well documented. In fact, you likely have someone in your immediate or extended family who is currently dealing with the fallout from a long-term care event. The question becomes, what's the best way to mitigate such an insidious risk?

Traditionally, there have only been three ways to do so:

1. **Self-Insure:** This requires accumulating a massive pile of money by the time you retire so you can afford to pay long-term care expenses for both you and your spouse out of pocket. While you may feel up to the task, this is not the most cost-effective way of neutralizing the risk. Keep

in mind that long-term care can cost between $7,000 and $9,000 per month, per person, depending on where you live. At that rate, you could burn through a lifetime of savings in just a few short years!

2. **Rely on Children:** While this is an option to which some couples resort, sad experience shows that children can resent having to take care of an aging parent. Furthermore, many children lack the time, energy, know-how, and resources to provide an appropriate level of care.

3. **Buy a Long-Term Care Policy:** Long-term care policies pay a benefit when, as determined by a doctor, the insured can no longer perform two of six activities of daily living—e.g., eating, bathing, dressing, toileting, transferring (walking), and continence.

Of the three above-mentioned alternatives, buying a long-term care policy may *seem* like the easiest way to mitigate the enormous risks associated with a long-term care event. But if that's the case, why have long-term care insurance sales all but dried up in recent years? There are three main reasons:

1. **Expense:** Long-term care insurance for a husband and wife can be cost prohibitive. Typical premiums for two 50-year-olds can run anywhere from $6,000 to $8,000 per year.

2. **Hard to Qualify:** Qualification for a long-term care policy is based on morbidity (likelihood that you'll need long-term care) rather than mortality (longevity). You might have a life expectancy of 120, but if you have a bad back, bad hip, bad knee, etc., you may be deemed "high risk" and fail to qualify for a policy.

3. **Use-It-or-Lose-It Proposition:** Most people despise paying for something they hope they never have to use. With traditional long-term care insurance, you could pay premiums for 25 years, but if you die peacefully in your sleep never having needed coverage, they won't return your money at the end. It will go to pay for someone else's long-term care. This use-it-or-lose-it scenario is enough to dissuade most people from ever entering into the arrangement.

A Fourth Alternative

Fortunately, there is an alternative way to protect your retirement savings from the drain of a long-term care event without all the heartburn that comes with traditional long-term care insurance. And that's by availing yourself of the benefits of—plug your ears, Dave and Suze—cash value life insurance. Once again, the permanent life insurance alternative that accomplishes this the most efficiently and effectively is Indexed Universal Life.

Here's how it works. If you purchase an IUL with what's called a chronic illness rider, you can access your death benefit in advance of your death for the purpose of paying for long-term care. For example, let's say you have a death benefit of $400,000 and have a long-term care event. Upon approval, the insurance company will send you 25% of your death benefit, or $100,000 per year, every year for four years for the purpose of paying for long-term care. Now, they may discount that benefit slightly based on the age in which you receive the benefit, but the point is this: they're willing to give you your death benefit while you're alive for the purpose of paying for long-term care. And should you die peacefully in your sleep 30 years from now never having needed long-term care, someone's still getting a death benefit, probably your kids or your grandkids! So, you'll never have that sensation of having paid for something you hope you never have to use.

The *Wall Street Journal*

Now, I'm not the only one who thinks that cash value life insurance is an attractive alternative when it comes to mitigating long-term care. In fact, the *Wall Street Journal* called it the most popular tool with which to mitigate the long-term care threat. According to a recent article, policies that

> combine long-term-care coverage with a potential life-insurance benefit are called "hybrids," and they are reshaping the long-term-care niche of the U.S. insurance industry just as it had appeared headed for obsolescence.[6]

---

6. Leslie Scism, "Long-Term-Care Insurance Isn't Dead. It's Now an Estate-Planning Tool," June 11, 2018, https://www.wsj.com/articles /long-term-care-insurance-isnt-dead-its-now-an-estate-planning -tool-1528387201.

Why are these "hybrid" policies reshaping the long-term care landscape? As it turns out, Americans simply don't like paying for coverage they *hope* they never have to use. They're far more comfortable with an approach that allows them to use their death benefit while they're alive, but pass those funds on to their heirs should they die never having needed long-term care.

Summary

Traditional long-term care insurance has long been the primary tool by which Americans have mitigated the long-term care threat. But it's an expensive approach, can be hard to qualify, and the insured is faced with a long-term, heartburn-inducing, use-it-or-lose-it premium payment. By availing yourself of an Indexed Universal Life policy with a chronic illness rider, however, you can mitigate the long-term care threat without all the angst that goes along with the traditional approach. You do pay for the coverage, but if you die peacefully in your sleep never having needed it, your heirs still get a death benefit, so there isn't that sensation of having paid for something you hope you never have to use. Far from the scam mainstream gurus claim it to be, cash value life insurance has become the go-to means by which a retiring generation of baby boomers mitigate the risk of long-term care.

CONTEXT #3: TAXABLE INVESTMENT ALTERNATIVE

If you've been following social media lately, chances are you've seen "finfluencers" making the case that Indexed Universal Life can outperform the stock market over time. They even go so far as to encourage you to recapture funds you're currently investing into Roth 401(k)s or Roth IRAs and redirect them to the IUL.

By marketing the IUL as a stock market alternative, however, they become massive targets upon which financial gurus rightly train their rhetorical cannons. A typical "IUL is better than the stock market" debunking might go as follows:

> Let's say you're a 35-year-old male who invests $20,000 per year into an IUL earning 6% net of fees over time. By the time you reach 65, you will have accumulated $1,676,033.
>
> Instead of contributing that $20,000 to an

IUL, let's redirect it to a stock-heavy allocation in your Roth 401(k). If we can grow those dollars at 9% net of fees over that same time frame, you will have instead accumulated $2,971,504.

	CONTRIBUTION	ROR	TOTAL
IUL	$20,000	6%	$1,676,033
Roth 401(k)	$20,000	9%	$2,971,504

In other words, that fateful decision to adopt the IUL over the Roth 401(k) would have cost you almost $1.3 million!

So, maybe Dave Ramsey was right when it comes to cash value life insurance? Do 100% of these policies suck 100% of the time? Not exactly. The truth is, the IUL was never designed to keep pace with the stock market. IULs from top carriers have historical track records of between 5% and 7% net of fees over time. Far from a stock alternative, an IUL could be much more accurately characterized as a bond alternative (more on this later).

Hold the Phone . . .

Even though I just made the case that IULs are *not* to be compared with equities, is there ever a scenario in which it *could* beat the stock market? Is there ever a context in which those social media finfluencers might actually be right? Surprisingly, the answer is yes.

Growing Money in Your Taxable Bucket

To demonstrate how an IUL might beat a stock market portfolio, let me put my own spin on an investing approach championed by Dave Ramsey himself. First, let's dig into the details of Ramsey's approach. According to Ramsey, you should begin by fully funding your Roth IRA and Roth 401(k). If you still have money left over, fully fund your Health Savings Account and then pay off your house. If you still have money left over to invest, here's what Ramsey recommends:

> *Lots of people assume that you can't invest in a mutual fund unless it's in an IRA or a 401(k).* Did you know you can open an investment account through a brokerage firm and put as

much money in it as you want? *And it's a good option if you have money left to save . . .*

The drawback of this kind of investment is obvious: you pay taxes on any money your account earns. When *you pay those taxes will vary, so we won't go into specifics here. Just know that Uncle Sam wants his money, so be ready for that.*[7]

As Dave points out, taxable brokerage accounts don't grow as productively as their tax-free counterparts, but short of buying an "onerous" and "clunky" cash value life insurance policy, what other alternatives do you have?

So, given Ramsey's vehement opposition to cash value life insurance, you decide to go all-in on the taxable brokerage account. For our example's sake, let's say that 100% of the growth on your money is taxed at short-term capital gains. That means that any gains you experience in that account will be piled right on top of all your other ordinary income and be taxed at your highest marginal tax bracket.

---

7. "Investing 2.0: Where Do I Invest Beyond Retirement," Ramsey Solutions, February 26, 2024, https://www.ramseysolutions.com/retirement/where-do-i-invest-beyond-15.

For our example's sake, let's also say that you have access to an IUL that can net you 6% average returns over time. The question becomes—is there ever a scenario in which you should opt for the IUL over the Dave Ramsey–recommended taxable brokerage account? Put differently, what pretax rate of return would you have to experience in your taxable stock market investments to beat the IUL growing at 6%?

To calculate this, we simply take the IUL's 6% net rate of return and divide it by 1 minus your marginal tax bracket. The formula looks like this:

$$\frac{.06}{1 - [\text{marginal tax bracket}]}$$

Let's run through the gamut of tax brackets to see how these two alternatives stack up.

If you were in the 22% tax bracket, we'd divide 6% by 1 minus 0.22 and get 7.69%. In other words, you'd only have to get 7.69% in your taxable brokerage account to outperform the IUL. If you believe you can earn 9% net of fees in that account, then the IUL loses.

All right, let's try the 24% tax bracket. If we divide

6% by 1 minus 0.24, that gives us a 7.89% rate of return. In other words, you'd only have to get 7.89% return in your taxable brokerage account to beat the IUL. Again, the 9% taxable investment still wins.

Okay, let's try the 32% tax bracket. Six percent divided by 1 minus 0.32 gets us all the way up to 8.82%. Nearly a wash!

Next, we try the 35% tax bracket. That gets us to 9.23%. In other words, if you believe the stock market can only deliver 9% over time, then the IUL is clearly the better alternative!

Finally, let's try the 37% tax bracket. That gets us to a gravity-defying, stratospheric 9.52%. Again, if you believe your taxable brokerage account can only net you

TAX BRACKET	TAX-FREE RATE OF RETURN	TAXABLE EQUIVALENT	WINNER
22%	6%	7.69%	Stocks
24%	6%	7.89%	Stocks
32%	6%	8.82%	Stocks
35%	6%	9.23%	IUL
37%	6%	9.52%	IUL

9%, then the IUL would grow your savings much more productively over time!

When you look at the above chart, you'll notice a clear trend. The higher your marginal tax bracket, the more it makes sense to contribute your surplus savings to an IUL over a taxable brokerage account.

What If I'm in a Lower Tax Bracket?

If you're in a lower tax bracket and you have surplus savings to invest, you shouldn't swear off the IUL altogether. Remember, if you can get 6% tax-free over time, that's still a safe and productive way to grow a portion of your assets. It just wouldn't replace the stock portion of your portfolio. In fact, in most scenarios, the IUL can be more accurately described as a *bond alternative*. Reach into your portfolio, remove the bonds, replace them with Indexed Universal Life, and you'll increase your return, lower your risk, lower the standard deviation of your entire portfolio, and experience a better outcome over time.

A Risky Proposition

Keep in mind that in order to get those high returns in your taxable brokerage account, you'll have to take a commensurate amount of stock market risk. Further, there are no guarantees you *will* experience those high rates of return. Given a few untimely down years in the market, your returns could fall well below 9%. And in those scenarios, the IUL wins.

The Flexibilities of the IUL

Now, not only are the IUL's tax-free returns superior to the after-tax stock market returns in those higher tax brackets, but the IUL has flexibilities that make it a dynamic tool with which to build tax-free wealth.

No Contribution Limits

First, there are no contribution limits. So, if you need to plow $50,000 or even $100,000 into your IUL per year, you can do it.

No Income Limitations

Unlike the Roth IRA, you aren't constrained by

income limitations. So, even if you breached the Roth's modified adjusted gross income limit of $240,000 (Married Filing Jointly), you could still contribute to the IUL.

Safe and Productive Growth

With the IUL, you can get that 6% tax-free rate of return without taking any more market risk than what you're accustomed to taking in your savings account. The IUL is the poster child for safe and productive growth.

A Death Benefit That Doubles as Long-Term Care

Don't forget that you can receive your death benefit in advance of your death for the purpose of paying for long-term care. And should you die never having needed it, your heirs will still get a death benefit.

Summary

Even though I wouldn't normally recommend an IUL as a stock market replacement, it can be an effective alternative when compared to the after-tax returns in a taxable brokerage account. Once again, the higher your marginal tax bracket, the more the calculus favors

Indexed Universal Life. And even if you're in a lower tax bracket, the IUL can be a very competitive bond alternative that has flexibilities that you won't find with any other tax-free alternative.

CONCLUSION

If you take most financial gurus at face value, there is never any context in which you should consider utilizing cash value life insurance as part of a balanced, comprehensive approach to tax-free retirement. Because of their one-size-fits-all, black-and-white financial planning worldview, permanent life insurance must either be praised or shunned entirely—there can be no middle ground. By blacklisting cash value life insurance, however, they deprive their follower of a dynamic tool that can purge a number of insidious risks from their retirement picture.

By using permanent life insurance as a Volatility Shield, for example, investors can dramatically increase the sustainable withdrawal rate on their stock market portfolios. In many cases this can help bridge a retirement shortfall that would otherwise force investors to resort to unsavory alternatives such as saving more, spending less, working longer, dying sooner, or taking more risks in the stock market.

By using life insurance as a means of neutralizing the long-term care risk, they can mitigate the heartburn associated with the use-it-or-lose-it approach of traditional long-term care insurance. Should the investor die peacefully in their sleep never having needed long-term care, their heirs still receive a death benefit.

And finally, life insurance can be used as a safe and productive alternative to investing surplus savings into a taxable brokerage account. When you calculate the after-tax equivalent return you'd have to get in your taxable investment, Indexed Universal Life proves to be the more productive alternative. Depending on your marginal tax bracket, its tax-free returns can often outstrip the after-tax returns in your taxable bucket, without all the stock market risk that goes along with it. Even if you're in a lower tax bracket, the IUL is a productive bond alternative that can help increase the return and lower the risk of your entire portfolio.

5

Case Study:
Accumulation Years

To this point I've shown that there's a yawning gap between what mainstream financial gurus recommend and the math-based solutions sophisticated investors require to maximize the efficiency of their retirement savings. By failing to bridge this gap with time-tested, customized financial advice, investors risk losing hundreds of thousands of dollars and running out of money years in advance of life expectancy.

In the next two chapters, I'll provide two case studies where I compare and contrast the guru-based approach and a customized, math-based, Power of Zero approach to growing and distributing wealth.

In this chapter, we'll be looking at the case study of Jack and Erin Brown. I'll start by examining their accumulation strategy through the lens of the guru-based retirement approach. I'll lay out the strategy a mainstream guru would likely recommend and explain the implications for the Browns' retirement. I'll then apply math-based, Power of Zero planning principles to their situation and demonstrate the long-term implications for their after-tax spendable cash flow in retirement.

CASE STUDY

The Browns' Financial Profile

General Information

Jack Brown: Age 45

Erin Brown: Age 45

Tax Filing Status: Married Filing Jointly

Jack's Job: Computer programmer

Jack's Income: $150,000

Erin's Job: Stay-at-home mom

Retirement age: 65

Marginal Tax Rate: 30% (combined state and federal)

Retirement Income Need (above what Social Security provides): $100,000 pretax starting at age 65, adjusted every year thereafter for inflation

Assets

Jack's 401(k) Balance: $230,000

Jack's 401(k) Contributions: $19,000

Jack's 401(k) Company Match: $4,500

Rate of Return: 7% net of fees

ARE THE BROWNS ON TRACK?

Before we delve into a comparison of alternatives, we must first answer this question: Are the Browns on track to meet their retirement goals according to traditional, mainstream guru benchmarks? In calculating this, we won't have the luxury of using Dave Ramsey's 12% returns and 8% withdrawal rates. This could mistakenly lead the Browns to believe that they are, in fact, saving enough money for retirement. We will instead utilize the more realistic variables commonly used by traditional gurus: a 7% growth rate and a 4% rate of withdrawal.

Given the Four Percent Rule and their $100,000 retirement need, the Browns would have to accumulate $2,500,000 by day-1 of retirement. Remember the formula we discussed earlier? Divide the retirement income need by the sustainable withdrawal rate and that tells you how much money you will need to accumulate by your retirement date. Given their current retirement balances of $230,000, the Browns will need to accumulate an additional $2,270,000 over the next 20 years to meet their retirement goal.

Given a 7% growth rate, however, the Browns will only have accumulated $1,850,000 by the time they retire. That means they have a gaping $650,000 hole in their retirement plan. Given this projected shortfall, they can resort to the five distasteful alternatives we discussed earlier.

Save More

In the guru-based model, the Browns would have to save more money. How much more? A whopping $16,000 per year. In other words, quit going out to eat, quit going on vacation, and pull back the belt a couple of notches so they can meet their retirement needs. That's a 10.6% reduction in the Browns' lifestyle today so they can achieve their retirement goals by age 65.

Spend Less

If the Browns don't see themselves saving more today, they could always agree to spend less in retirement. Based on the $1,850,000 they will have saved by the time they retire, and given a 4% sustainable withdrawal rate, they would only be able to spend $74,000 per year in retirement, adjusted each year thereafter for inflation. This represents a 26% reduction in their original retirement income goal. Ouch!

Work Longer

This option involves pushing their retirement date back until age 69 so that their assets have more time to grow and compound. This would also shorten the amount of time over which their assets would be required to last.

Die Sooner

Again, I offer this alternative somewhat in jest. But assuming they had a $1,850,000 balance at retirement and wanted to take the full $100,000 annual distribution, adjusted each year for inflation, they'd only be able to make those withdrawals for 15 years with a reasonably high likelihood of not running out of money. Not exactly the foolproof, heartburn-free strategy the Browns are searching for.

Take More Risks in the Stock Market

The last of the traditional, guru-endorsed alternatives to bridge their retirement shortfall is to take more risks in the stock market. In other words, they need to shoot for a higher rate of return. Instead of growing their money at 7%, they'd have to grow it closer to 9%. But taking more risks doesn't necessarily guarantee the Browns will achieve that 9% average return over time. More risk means wider swings in the market and raises the possibility that the Browns could miss their retirement goals by an even wider margin.

SUMMARY

In summary, under the traditional, guru-endorsed model (Dave Ramsey excluded), the Browns can bridge their retirement shortfall by saving more, spending less, working longer, dying sooner, or taking more risks with their investments. And with this last alternative, they could, in theory, run out of money even faster.

THE VOLATILITY SHIELD: INDEXED UNIVERSAL LIFE

In the last chapter, I explained how Indexed Universal Life is a proven way to shield your stock market investments from volatility in retirement. When funded properly and deployed strategically, it can as much as double your sustainable withdrawal rate over time.

Once again, to pull this off, the Browns would need to accumulate at least three years' worth of living expenses in their IUL by day-1 of retirement. Once retired, they would pay for their living expenses out of their life insurance cash value in the years following a down year in their stock market portfolio. This gives their stock portfolio a chance to recover before they take further withdrawals. By doing so, they can as much as double their sustainable distribution rate in retirement.

THE POWER OF ZERO RECOMMENDATION

I'd begin by recommending that Jack reduce his current $19,000 contribution in his 401(k) down to the 3% match. That means that both he and his employer would be contributing $4,500 per year for a total of $9,000. That frees up $14,500 per year. Because that's a pretax number, we would then have to pay a combined state and federal tax rate of 30%. That leaves us with $10,150 to contribute to an Indexed Universal Life policy on Jack on an annual basis. He'd continue to make those contributions every year until the Browns reach 65. By the time they retire, Jack will have accumulated just over $350,000 in his IUL's cash value. That would be enough to fund five full years of *after-tax* living expenses.

A TRIP TO MONTE CARLO

According to my Monte Carlo simulations, if the Browns can pay for five years' worth of living expenses out of their IUL's cash value in the years following a down year in the market during the first decade of their retirement, an astounding thing happens. They are no longer constrained by the Four Percent Rule. They can now take 8% withdrawals on their retirement balances with 93% confidence that their money would last for a full 30-year retirement.

NOW HOLD ON A SECOND . . .

Hold the phone, you may be thinking. If the Browns take money that was destined for their 401(k) and earmark it for an Indexed Universal Life insurance policy, they *would* have five years' worth of living expenses accumulated by retirement. However, they would also have much *less* in their 401(k). In fact, instead of having

$1,850,000 in their 401(k), the Browns would have only $1,260,000. However, if they can now safely take 8% withdrawal rates on their 401(k) in retirement, their overall income is dramatically higher. Don't believe me? Let's do the math. An 8% withdrawal rate on their $1,260,000 401(k) balance would yield $100,800 of income per year, adjusted every year thereafter for inflation! In other words, by using their IUL as a Volatility Shield, the Browns would end up with less money in their 401(k) at retirement, but they'd now be able to take much *larger* sustainable distributions over the course of their retirement.

CONCLUSION

If we take to heart what Dave Ramsey, Suze Orman, Clark Howard, and Ramit Sethi tell us about cash value life insurance, we should avoid it at all costs. It isn't a serious investment alternative and could therefore never play a serious role in a viable retirement strategy. Moreover, if an advisor ever brings it up, you are to never work with that person again (Orman). Why? Because 100% of cash value sucks 100% of the time (Ramsey)!

By not utilizing cash value life insurance, however, the Browns would be facing a dramatic retirement shortfall. To bridge that gap under the traditional guru-based approach, they'd be forced to save more, spend less, work longer, die sooner, or take more risks in the stock market.

If the Browns look beyond the one-size-fits-all, paint-by-numbers guru approach to retirement, however, a whole new vista of possibilities begins to emerge. By simply incorporating Indexed Universal Life into their retirement strategy, they can as much as double their sustainable withdrawal rate in retirement and dramatically increase the likelihood that their retirement savings will last through life expectancy. Furthermore, they'll have a death benefit they can receive in advance of their death for the purpose of paying for long-term care.

6
Case Study:
Distribution Years

In the last chapter I made the case that if you stick to the guru-endorsed approach to bridging your retirement shortfall you'll have to resort to some painful, angst-inducing alternatives to reach your retirement goals. I then showed how proven, Power of Zero principles can help increase your sustainable withdrawal rate in order to meet your retirement income needs. In this chapter, I'm going to apply traditional, guru-based advice to a couple who is much closer to their retirement date. How would their retirement unfold were they to adhere to the traditional, guru-based model? Conversely, how much better off could they be if they implemented the Power of Zero strategies I've outlined thus far in this book?

WHICH GURU'S ADVICE DO WE IMPLEMENT?

Once again, since advice can vary wildly from guru to guru, I can't simply lay out a *definitive* guru model for the purposes of this comparison. For example, Dave Ramsey says you can take 8% sustainable withdrawals while Ken Fisher says you must adhere to the Four

Percent Rule.[1] So, in this section, we must choose the combination of recommendations that most embody the guru-based approach to sustainable distributions in retirement.

Here's the guru advice we'll use in our comparison:

Investment Allocation: Use stocks *and* bonds (Fisher, Orman, Howard, Sethi)

Sustainable Withdrawal Rate: 4% (Fisher, Orman, Howard, Sethi)

Annuities: Not on your life! (Fisher, Howard, Ramsey, Orman, Sethi)

Roth Conversions: Not within five years of retirement! (Ramsey)

Cash Value Life Insurance: You're kidding, right? (Ramsey, Orman, Sethi, Howard)

Now, you may be thinking that it isn't fair to utilize the most deficient aspects of each guru's retirement approach when drawing comparisons, but you have to remember the point of this exercise. My goal is to

---

1. "Fisher Investments: Why You Should Say No to 'Income Investing,'" n.d., https://www.reuters.com/plus/fisher-investments -why-you-should-say-no-to-income-investing.

advance the dialogue around sustainable retirement strategies in retirement. And I can only do that by contrasting the guru-based approach, however defective and misguided it may at times be, with the proven, math-based, Power of Zero strategy that disciplined, sophisticated investors require to maximize their cash flow in retirement.

Now that we've established the guru-based advice parameters we'll be using for our comparison, let's dig into the financial profile of our next case study, Norm and Clara Johnson.

CASE STUDY

The Johnsons' Financial Profile
General Information
Norm Johnson: Age 62
Clara Johnson: Age 62
Retirement Date: 67
Tax Filing Status: Married Filing Jointly

Norm's Job: Accountant

Clara's Job: Administrative Assistant

Retirement Income Need: $100,000 pretax starting at 67, adjusted for inflation each year thereafter

Assets

Norm's IRA: $800,000

Norm's 401(k) Balance: $200,000

Norm's 401(k) Contribution: $10,000

Norm's 401(k) Match: $5,000

Rate of Return: 7% net of fees

Combined Social Security: $40,000 per year starting at 67

Long-Term Care Insurance: none

Cash Value Life Insurance: none

THE GURU APPROACH

The guru-based approach for the Johnsons is relatively straightforward, particularly since no annuities or life insurance can be incorporated into the plan. And given the Ramsey-enforced prohibition on Roth conversions within five years of retirement, we won't have to account for any tax-saving strategies.

Sustainable Withdrawal Rates

Given the outright prohibition on annuities, the Johnsons are forced to rely on the stock market approach to purging longevity risk from their portfolio. In other words, to have a high likelihood that their money will last through their actuarial life expectancy, they must constrain themselves to a small withdrawal rate over the course of their retirement. How small? That's where the Four Percent Rule comes into play. As a reminder, the Four Percent Rule dictates that you can only ever withdraw 4% of your day-1 retirement balance, adjusted each year thereafter for inflation. For example, assuming the Johnsons' $1,000,000 grows at 7% per year between now and age 67, they would have $1,488,812 at retirement. That means they could withdraw 4% of that amount, or $59,552 ($1,488,812 x .04 = $59,552), that first year. If their lifestyle calls for $100,000 and Social Security provides $40,000, then they will have just about met that requirement ($59,552 + $40,000 = $99,552)!

A Fly in the Ointment

Right about now, you may be thinking to yourself: *Wow, the Johnsons really nailed it! They need $60,000 pretax above and beyond what Social Security provides, and their retirement balance of $1,488,812 at age 67 will essentially meet that need based on the Four Percent Rule. The Johnsons are all set for a long, happy, sustainable retirement journey. Score one for the gurus! What could possibly go wrong?!*

Well, I'd be happy to spell out precisely what could (and is likely to) go wrong. The Johnsons' plan doesn't account for three crucial factors, any one of which could send their retirement plan cartwheeling off the tracks. Those factors are:

1. Tax rate risk
2. Long-term care risk
3. Discretionary expenditures

Let's tackle each of these issues one by one.

#1. Tax Rate Risk

Sixty thousand dollars pretax at age 67 *could* be perfectly adequate to meet the Johnsons' lifestyle needs based on *today's* tax rates. But if tax rates were to rise dramatically, as many experts predict, then their after-tax income could fall well short of what their lifestyle requires.

For example, let's assume that in their first year of retirement, their combined state and federal effective tax rate is 25%. That means the after-tax withdrawal from their IRA will be $45,000. However, if what former US comptroller general David M. Walker says comes true, and tax rates double to pay for our nation's debt and unfunded entitlements, now we're looking at a combined state and federal tax rate of 50%. At that point, they'd only be netting $30,000 after-tax. And how will the Johnsons plug that $15,000 hole in their retirement income? If they're like most Americans, they'll end up taking even more money out of their IRAs and 401(k)s, in clear violation of the Four Percent Rule. And this, of course, will dramatically increase the likelihood that they'll run out of money before they run out of life. Again, in order for the Four Percent Rule to work, it must be obeyed with Zen-like precision. The minute you exceed the Four Percent Rule, you violate the mathematical framework that upholds it.

Now, if the Johnsons were to do a Roth conversion, in stark violation of Dave Ramsey's advice, they could lock in their taxes at historically low tax rates. Even if tax rates do rise dramatically in the future, they will have done all the heavy lifting beforehand and can take those dollars out 100% tax-free.

#2. Long-Term Care Risk

As we discussed in chapter 4, a long-term care event is one of the most insidious events that could ever befall your retirement plan, and the Johnsons are 100% exposed to it. Should Norm, for example, end up needing long-term care, almost all the money Clara was planning on spending in retirement now gets earmarked for the long-term care facility. She would get to keep:

- One house
- One car
- A Minimum Monthly Maintenance Needs Allowance (MMMNA) of about $2,500 per month
- About $130,000 of cash

So, what was shaping up to be a perfectly well-funded retirement for Clara turns into basic, subsistence-type living for the rest of her life. And, of course, the converse would hold true if Clara ended up needing long-term care.

#3. Discretionary Expenditures

Discretionary expenditures in retirement are any expenses above and beyond your basic lifestyle needs. They generally come in two flavors:

1. **Shock Expenses:** These are unexpected expenses that have the potential to turn your world upside down. You may have an unanticipated health care expense, need to replace the roof, or have to loan a family member money in a moment of need.
2. **Aspirational Expenses:** These are the wants of retirement, not the needs. These may include taking your grandkids to Disney World, buying a boat, or taking a trip around the world.

Unfortunately, the Four Percent Rule does not account for either type of discretionary expenditure.

For example, while $1,488,812 at age 67 may be enough to meet the Johnsons' lifestyle needs based on the Four Percent Rule, they won't have any money left to pay for discretionary expenditures. Were they to dig into that $1,488,812 to pay for those discretionary needs, they'd violate the Four Percent Rule and increase the likelihood of exhausting their resources prior to life expectancy.

THE POWER OF ZERO APPROACH

The Power of Zero approach shields the Johnsons from the impact of higher taxes, mitigates the long-term care risk, and gives them a pool of money from which to pay for discretionary expenses over the arc of a full 30-year retirement.

The Power of Zero strategy solves these traditional retirement threats by utilizing financial tools that have been specifically blacklisted by every guru we've thus far discussed. The tools I'm referring to are, you guessed it, annuities and cash value life insurance. So, for the following section, I'm asking that you cast aside any of your guru-based preconceptions and focus on a math-based solution that dramatically increases the likelihood that the Johnsons will have a successful retirement.

THE STRATEGY

Any improvement upon the guru-based approach begins by kicking the Four Percent Rule to the curb and embracing a guaranteed lifetime income approach. Remember, at the end of the day, we're looking for the most cost-effective way to purge longevity risk from the Johnsons' retirement picture. As a reminder, the Four Percent Rule is almost always the most expensive way of doing so. If you recall, to bridge their $60,000 income gap at age 67, all $1,488,812 of their liquid retirement savings will be claimed by the Four Percent Rule. Using a guaranteed lifetime income annuity, conversely, they can accomplish the same thing for much less money.

The Right Kind of Annuity

Before we get into how much of the Johnsons' retirement savings might be allocated toward an annuity, we must first identify the right kind. Remember, there are two huge risks we're trying to purge from the Johnsons' retirement plan: longevity risk *and* tax-rate risk. For reasons I'll soon discuss, the annuity that best mitigates both of these risks is a Fixed Indexed Annuity (FIA).

Mitigating Longevity Risk

The FIA neutralizes longevity risk by providing you a lifetime income rider that, once elected, gives you guaranteed, inflation-adjusted income that will continue to flow into your bank account so long as you're on this side of the grass. Not only does the FIA help you mitigate longevity risk, but it also neutralizes the subset of risks that it amplifies. Again, these risks include sequence of return risk, withdrawal rate risk, inflation risk, and long-term care risk.

Mitigating Tax-Rate Risk

If you want to shield your guaranteed lifetime income from the impact of higher taxes, you must have the flexibility of doing a Roth conversion. Now, every FIA company allows you to do a Roth conversion. Unfortunately, most require you to execute that Roth conversion all in one year. This is a deal-breaker of the highest order. Here's why. Let's say you're in the 22% marginal tax bracket and convert your entire $500,000 IRA annuity to Roth, all in one year. All of that $500,000 will be piled right on top of your other income and be taxed at your highest marginal tax bracket. That means you will pay tax on a large portion of that Roth conversion at the higher tax rates, including the highest of them all: 37%. Throw in another 6% for state, and now we're talking 43%. In an effort to avoid a doubling of tax rates over time, you doubled your tax bracket in the short term!

That's why you must insist that your FIA have what I referred to earlier as a *Piecemeal Internal Roth Conversion* feature. This allows you to convert your annuity to Roth in an amount of your choosing over a time frame that your financial plan calls for. You'll be able to convert your annuity slowly enough that you don't rise into a tax bracket that gives you heartburn, but quickly enough that you get all the heavy lifting done before tax rates go up for good.

Contribution to the Fixed Indexed Annuity

Now that we understand which type of annuity we'll be utilizing to bridge the Johnsons' retirement income gap, let's discuss how much money we'll be earmarking toward the annuity itself. Remember, we're trying to provide a guaranteed, inflation-adjusted stream of income that can forever purge longevity risk *and* tax-rate risk from their retirement picture. Based on prevailing interest rates at the writing of this book, the Johnsons would need to contribute $600,000 of Norm's IRA to a Fixed Indexed Annuity with a Piecemeal Internal Roth Conversion feature. Given a modest growth rate of 5% per year, that would produce $60,000 of pretax income at age 67, adjusted every year thereafter for inflation.[2]

In other words, by earmarking 60% of their $1,000,000 of retirement savings, the Johnsons can forever purge longevity risk from their retirement outlook. And, by executing a Piecemeal Internal Roth Conversion along the way, they can likewise purge tax-rate risk from their golden years. Remember, they will pay tax, but they'll do so at historically low tax rates along the way!

Mitigating Long-Term Care Risk Without the Heartburn

By utilizing the FIA, we knocked out longevity risk and tax-rate risk much less expensively than by way of the Four Percent Rule. The Four Percent Rule would have

---

2. The growth of the lifetime income is linked to the upward movement of an underlying stock market index, which, if history serves as a model, is likely to keep pace with inflation.

consumed their entire $1,488,812 portfolio at age 67 ($1,000,000 grown at 7% per year until age 67). By peeling off $600,000 at age 62 and contributing it to a Fixed Indexed Annuity, their retirement income needs will be fully covered at age 67.

By neutralizing longevity risk far less expensively than the traditional, guru-endorsed approach, the Johnsons now have $400,000, some of which can be used to purge long-term care risk from their retirement picture.

Indexed Universal Life

Here is where I'd once again recommend that the Johnsons avail themselves of that most verboten of all financial tools: cash value life insurance in the form of Indexed Universal Life. Why would I recommend a financial tool that's universally condemned by every guru we've thus far discussed? Because it accomplishes something that no other financial tool can accomplish. It mitigates long-term care risk without the heartburn associated with traditional use-it-or-lose-it long-term care insurance. Remember, certain IUL carriers allow you to receive your death benefit in advance of your death for the purpose of paying for long-term care. And should you die peacefully in your sleep 30 years from now never having needed long-term care, someone's still getting a death benefit, probably your kids or your grandkids! So, there isn't that sensation of having paid for something you hope you never have to use.

For the purpose of mitigating long-term care risk from the Johnsons' retirement picture, I recommend they each have IULs with death benefits of $400,000. Were they to need long-term care, the insurance company would send them 25% of that death benefit per year, every year, for four years for the purpose of paying for it.[3] That would require that they allocate a total of $35,000 per year for five years to their IULs.

Discretionary Expenses

As you may recall, one of the huge pitfalls of the Four Percent Rule is that the Johnsons would have no surplus money with which to pay for discretionary expenses in retirement. Every last bit of their $1,488,812 at age 67 would be claimed by the Four Percent Rule. If they

---

3. Insurance companies may discount this amount based on the age at which you receive the benefit.

violate this rule in order to pay for their discretionary expenses, they increase the likelihood of running out of money before they die.

By utilizing the FIA, however, they free up an additional $400,000. The Johnsons' IULs would claim $175,000, leaving them $225,000 to grow and compound between now and when they retire. If they can continue to grow that money at 7% between now and age 67, they will have accumulated $315,574.

Supercharge Your Discretionary Spending!

So not only have the Johnsons purged tax-rate risk, longevity risk, and long-term care risk from their retirement picture, but they have an extra $315,574 with which to pay for discretionary expenses!

But the good news doesn't end there. By properly funding the Johnsons' IULs, we maximize their cash value growth over time. To properly fund their IUL, they'll need to buy as little death benefit as the IRS requires and stuff as much money in as the IRS allows. If the Johnsons allow their IULs to grow and compound for 10 years, they will have built up a substantial pool of tax-free cash that can be spent in year 11 and beyond. If, instead of taking money out of their liquid investments to pay for discretionary expenses in the year following a down year in the market, they pay for those expenses out of their IULs, their discretionary funds last much longer. Not only can their IULs mitigate long-term care risk, but they can neutralize volatility along the way. Talk about doing double duty!

CONCLUSION

In this chapter's case study, I showed that by utilizing a Fixed Indexed Annuity, the Johnsons could neutralize longevity risk much less expensively than by relying on the guru-endorsed Four Percent Rule. Furthermore, by using an FIA with a Piecemeal Internal Roth Conversion feature, they can systematically convert that IRA annuity to Roth to shield it from the threat of higher taxes in the future.

Lastly, by choosing a guaranteed lifetime income annuity over the Four Percent Rule, the Johnsons free up a substantial sum of money that can be earmarked for two IUL policies that can help insulate them from the long-term care risk. They can then invest their remaining savings in the stock market to help pay for discretionary expenses over the balance of their retirement. And since their IULs can also serve as a Volatility Shield, they dramatically increase the likelihood that those discretionary funds will last as long as they do.

It's important to note that none of these additional benefits would be available had the Johnsons adopted the guru-based approaches discussed in this book. By eschewing annuities and cash value life insurance, they would have been forced to live out their retirement under the tyranny of the Four Percent Rule. Furthermore, the guru approach would have consumed their entire net worth, exposing them to long-term care risk and depriving them of a pool of discretionary funds that is so indispensable to a happy, stress-free retirement.

7
A Final Word

As this book draws to a close, I must repeat that this was *not* intended to be a financial guru hit piece. It's merely my best, good-faith effort to advance the dialogue around sustainable retirement planning principles. Again, Dave Ramsey, Suze Orman, and the other gurus we've discussed in this book have proven to be invaluable resources for a huge swath of America that struggles with debt and can't seem to get off square one when it comes to saving for retirement.

All that said, there's no hiding the fact that the retirement advice they dispense tends to be good for bad investors and bad for good investors. If you're a sophisticated, disciplined investor, adopting these gurus' strategies could cost you hundreds of thousands of dollars, expose you to a vast array of retirement risks, and force you to run out of money years in advance of life expectancy. If you fall into this category, I hope this book helped bridge the gap between the advice these gurus provide and the specific, time-tested, math-based, Power of Zero advice your retirement plan requires.

WAIT, AREN'T *YOU* A GURU OF SORTS?

Now, at this point, you may be asking the question: "Hey, Dave, don't *you* fancy yourself a financial guru? And if so, who's to say *I* should heed *your* advice!" These are both fair questions. After all, maybe *I'm* falling into the same types of guru traps I discuss in this book. To be clear, I don't hold myself out to be a financial guru in the general sense. My goal isn't to reach every single American, as is the case with Dave Ramsey or Suze Orman. Instead, I hope to connect with a narrow swath of Americans who have saved well but are looking to maximize their after-tax cash flow in retirement. Simply put, my message is for financially disciplined investors who feel like the broad-based, one-size-fits-all advice dispensed by the traditional guru community is either wrong, misguided, or devoid of the specific strategy required to fully optimize their retirement plan.

NEXT STEPS

If the message of this book has resonated with you, you may be wondering about next steps. Now that we've dispelled the guru myths and filled in the guru gaps, how do you apply this information to your specific financial situation? There are two separate paths along which you may choose to proceed. The course you ultimately choose is entirely up to you!

Go It Alone!

The first path is what I call the "Go It Alone" approach. This involves gathering as much information as you can and becoming a student of tax-free retirement planning. In this approach, *you* become the guru. If this is the path you choose to take, I might recommend several additional resources for your retirement planning journey. For starters, I suggest you go back and read *The Power of Zero*. This is my first, groundbreaking book that precipitated the entire Power of Zero retirement revolution. In this book I make the case that taxes, even 10 years from now, are likely to be dramatically higher than they are today. I then identify the three basic buckets of money within which you can save retirement dollars: taxable, tax-deferred, and tax-free. I then make the case that in a rising tax rate environment there is a mathematically perfect amount of money to have in the taxable and tax-deferred buckets. Anything above and beyond these ideal amounts should be systematically shifted to tax-free.

I'd then recommend moving to *Look Before You LIRP*. In *The Power of Zero* I introduce the concept of cash value life insurance, or what I refer to as the Life Insurance Retirement Plan (LIRP), as an integral part of a balanced, comprehensive approach to tax-free retirement. In *Look Before You LIRP*, I make the case that not all LIRPs are created equal. I also explain why Indexed Universal Life is the LIRP that gives you the highest chance of reaching your retirement goals within the Power of Zero framework. Furthermore, I explain how not all IULs are created equal and why you need to be armed with a laundry list of attributes as you investigate IUL alternatives.

The next book on your list should be *The Volatility Shield*. This financial novella couches the volatility shield strategy within a fast-paced, heartwarming, suspenseful story with a cool, M. Night Shyamalan twist ending. After finishing this story, you'll emerge with a deeper understanding of cash value life insurance and how it can liberate you from the shackles of the Four Percent Rule.

Lastly, I'd recommend you read *Tax-Free Income for Life*. In this book I explain how, historically, you could mitigate either longevity risk or tax-rate risk, but never both within the same financial plan. For example, if you wanted to mitigate longevity risk, you had to tie your money up in illiquid annuities that made Roth conversions all but impossible. Conversely, if you wanted to mitigate tax-rate risk, you had to leave your money in liquid investments that left you completely exposed to longevity risk. By introducing the concept of the Fixed Indexed Annuity with a Piecemeal Internal Roth Conversion feature, I show how you can mitigate both longevity risk and tax-rate risk within the very same retirement strategy.

Outside of these four additional books, I'd strongly recommend you listen to my weekly *Power of Zero* podcast and YouTube channel where I:

- Address the current fiscal trajectory of our country
- Discuss Power of Zero strategy
- Challenge the misguided advice of, you guessed it, financial gurus

If you do choose to become your own tax-free retirement planning guru, then I think you'll find my books, podcast, and YouTube channel to be timely, insightful resources that arm you with all the knowledge you'll need to navigate your way to the 0% tax bracket in retirement.

I Need Some Help!

If, after reviewing the tax-free retirement strategies I discuss in this or any of my other books you determine you need a steady hand to guide you along the way, I'm happy to be a resource. Go to davidmcknight.com and click on the "Connect with an Advisor" button and I'd be delighted to refer you to a Power of Zero advisor in your neck of the woods who has been trained, vetted, and qualified personally by me. They'll answer any questions you may have and create a Before-and-After Comparison demonstrating the mathematical benefits of adopting a zero-tax approach to retirement planning. They'll also lay out a specific, step-by-step road map on how to get to the 0% tax bracket.

Learn more at davidmcknight.com.

ACKNOWLEDGMENTS

I'd like to begin by thanking the financial gurus featured in this book. Their contributions to the personal finance discussion have given me the opportunity to provide counterpoints that help advance the dialogue around sustainable retirement planning solutions. We're all after the same goal, and that's helping Americans wring the most efficiency out of their retirement savings. And though my criticisms of their strategies are at times sharp, there is no denying the positive role they've played in helping promote financial literacy across the country.

Special thanks go to the dedicated followers of the Power of Zero retirement philosophy. Your engagement with my books, YouTube videos, and podcast helps make books like this possible.

I am also immensely grateful to the legions of financial advisors who have read my books, embraced the tax-free retirement paradigm, and helped communicate it to their clients. They advocate tax-free planning principles in a world where tax-deferred saving is still the norm. Thank you for playing a pivotal role in this retirement planning revolution.

I'd also like to thank Certified Financial Planner™ professionals Kyle Swan and Greg Gillis for their thorough and thoughtful review of this manuscript. Their insights and feedback helped sharpen the book's message and smooth out its rough edges.

Thanks to my agent Howard Yoon for being a willing and reliable sounding board as I developed the concept for this book over the course of the last year.

Also, a huge thanks to the team at Matt Holt Books for believing in this project and helping bring it to life. I am particularly indebted to Matt Holt, Katie Dickman, Lydia Choi, Brigid Pearson, Ariel Jewett, and Michael Fedison.

Most importantly, I'd like to thank my wife, Felice, who, over the last 24 years, has been my steadfast companion and greatest inspiration. Without her, none of this is possible or worthwhile.

ABOUT THE AUTHOR

David McKnight graduated from Brigham Young University with honors in 1997. Over the past 27 years David has helped put thousands of Americans on the road to the zero percent tax bracket. He has made frequent appearances in *Forbes*, *USA Today*, the *New York Times*, Fox Business, CBS Radio, Bloomberg Radio, Huffington Post, Reuters, CNBC, Yahoo Finance, Nasdaq.com, Investor's Business Daily, Kiplinger's, MarketWatch, and numerous other national publications. His bestselling book *The Power of Zero* has sold over 400,000 copies and the updated and revised version was published by Penguin Random House. When it was launched in September 2018, it finished the week as the #2 most-sold business book in the world. For two consecutive years *Forbes* magazine has ranked *The Power of Zero* as a top-10 financial resource in the country. This book was recently made into a full-length documentary film entitled *The Power of Zero: The Tax Train Is Coming*. When David's follow-up book, *Tax-Free Income for Life* launched in November 2020, it finished the week as the #3 top-selling business book in the world. David and his wife Felice have seven children.

Want to connect with a
Power of Zero advisor?

Go to davidmcknight.com

@DavidMcKnight

@mcknightandco

The Power of Zero Show

@davidcmcknight